Lea

His ×

FAINT
Whispers

Bonnie!
I love you!
Cookie.

Jan 15.16

Published by Redemption Press, PO Box 427, Enumclaw, WA 98022

Toll Free (844) 2REDEEM (273-3336)

Redemption Press is honored to present this title in partnership with the author. The views expressed or implied in this work are those of the author. Redemption Press provides our imprint seal representing design excellence, creative content, and high quality production.

ISBN 13: 978-1-68314-606-3 (Paperback)
       978-1-68314-607-0 (ePub)
       978-1-68314-608-7 (Mobi)

Library of Congress Catalog Card Number: 2018952665

Learning to Discern
His Still, Small Voice

FAINT

Whispers

TAMMY LYONS
WILKINSON

REDEMPTION
PRESS

DEDICATION

To every person who has asked me, "How can I hear the voice of God?" I pray you develop a hunger and a thirst for His Word and His "voice" as you have never experienced before. As you seek God, I pray your relationship with Him will be strengthened and deepened.

God took a simple act of kindness and a viral video to spark a conversation. Without those events, this book would not exist. Thank you to each one of you who liked, commented, or shared the video.

> *My God,* I pray I have fulfilled your Scripture in Psalm 45:1: "My tongue is the pen of a skillful writer." I pray you would anoint this book and use it to the furtherance of your kingdom.

TABLE OF CONTENTS

⟶ FOREWORD ⟵

Her voice.

There is no mistaking the voice of Tammy Wilkinson. If you close your eyes and listen to her speak, you may dare venture to say that she is a bubbly ten-year-old, ponytail-swinging, hand-gesture-flying little girl from "somewhere mid-America."

But open your eyes and to your delight and surprise, you will find that all her contagious, childlike bubbliness resides deep within an electric-blue-eyed, Jesus-loving, people-serving, heart-surrendered mature woman of God.

I was near dozing off on my couch one afternoon, when out of the blue, I heard my friend Tammy's voice coming from my child's cell phone while she was scrolling through several social media videos. I flew up from my pillow, shouting, "Wait a minute! I know *that* voice. Play that video again!"

And as the video replayed Tammy's now Facebook-sensation video, "A Homeless Man, Chicken, and a Banana," I smiled, watching my friend unveil her heart-wrenching story of listening to God as He prompted her to feed a homeless man. I was amazed at her transparency, watching tears stream from her face as she shared her story. And I counted; not just one million, not even five million, but twelve million viewers were listening to her story.

Without a moment's hesitation, I leaped from my couch, grabbed my cell phone, and called her. Before she could even answer the phone with her usual "Hello, sunshine!" salutation, I blurted out, "Remember a few years ago, when I told you at our Nashville women's retreat that God had a ministry for you and that you would be speaking before thousands? Girl! This is *it*! It's here! I'm sitting here watching your video! Wow!"

Tammy's response was the same as always, "God is *awesome*."

Is it any wonder that the remaining hour and a half of our conversation sounded like two barnyard turkeys gobbling simultaneously from excitement?

Yes, God *is* awesome. And isn't it awesome how He has led you to this book? Like the homeless man in Tammy's story, God has a special word for you today too.

Sheri Thrower

Author of *My Will Be Done* and *Miracles in Room 107*
Founder and Director of SingAkadamie
Worship Leader for Ann Downing's Middle Tennessee
Women's Retreat, Nashville, Tennessee

INTRODUCTION

On December 14, 2016, I posted my first-ever Facebook Live video. I did not know it then, but my life would be forever changed. Posting that video was a simple act of obedience. God spoke, I heard, and I obeyed. Nothing more and nothing less. But God chose to take that simple act and magnify it in a way in which my mind could never have conceived! In just twenty-four hours, the video was viewed over eight million times, garnering the attention of news and radio personalities as well as movers and shakers such as Reba McEntire, Marcus Stanley, Taye Diggs, and Todd Chrisley.

It wasn't just the big names who heard and responded—after all, I'm not a big name; I'm a person just like you. And people just like us responded too.

I received messages from all over the world. Those messages ranged from a simple but heartfelt thank you to the sharing of a personal story of homelessness.

Three individuals shared personal and tragic stories. All three told me they had chosen the very day the video posted as the day on which they would end their lives.

Because they saw the love of Christ for a homeless man, they chose instead to seek out God's love.

My heart was overwhelmed with what was happening.

What *was* God doing?

Over the course of the following weeks as I read and studied, God began to reveal a common thread woven among the comments and personal messages pouring in through Facebook. Many people—maybe you were one of them—asked a simple question. "How do you hear the voice of God? You seem so sure it was Him, but how do you really know it was Jesus?"

My answer, which seemed very simple to me at the time, was, "My sheep listen to my voice, and I know them, and they follow me." That's John 10:27, and it became my standard answer. I did not know how else to explain it. For me, it was just that easy.

When I recorded the Facebook Live video, I'd had a relationship with Christ for twenty-two years. It had become second nature for me to recognize that voice, and I had learned to trust and obey it.

I learned in the days, weeks, and months that followed that not everyone understood what I was talking about when I spoke of recognizing God's voice. Many genuinely wanted to get to know Jesus the way I did.

It's my desire that you hear from Him too. I'd like to make learning to hear His voice easy for you. In the following pages, I hope to lead you in such a way that you find an answer to the question, "How do I hear the voice of God?" In John 10:27, Jesus refers to us as sheep who know His voice. I pray that as you read this book, you'll begin to understand that God does still talk to His people, but not all hear Him the same way.

I will show you many of the ways God's people hear His voice. I desire that you, too, find a deeper relationship with Jesus and the reassurance that comes from recognizing His voice.

I will be sharing stories from Ray Carman, a shepherd from the hills of Tennessee. He has given me much insight into the life of his flock as it compares to the everyday life of a Christian. I am excited to share his stories with you, with his permission, as they relate to hearing the voice of our Father.

Before you begin, I would ask that first you pray and invite the Lord Jesus to open your heart and your mind to receive whatever He would like to share with you, whatever He would have you receive from the words of this book.

> *Father God*, I thank you for this journey, and I thank you for choosing me to help others hear your voice. Without you, I am nothing. With you, I can be everything you have created me to be. Amen.

ONE

HE CHOSE ME: A LOOK AT THE HEART

In one moment, my life changed forever.

There was nothing extraordinary about the beginning of that day, nothing to hint that anything was going to be different. It was just another cold, blustery December day in New Castle, Indiana. The temperature hovered somewhere around twenty degrees, and there was about two inches of snow on the ground.

I shivered and pulled my coat closer as I slid into my car at the office to drive to the grocery store and pick up some gift cards. As I made my way into the store early that afternoon, I noticed a homeless man in a large overcoat huddled on a bench between the two sets of doors, obviously trying to keep warm, an overstuffed backpack by his side. He seemed to be in his midfifties and had dusky skin and rough hands with deep grooves.

We had no interpersonal exchange. I didn't even make eye contact with this man. I was focused on buying the gift cards and getting back to work.

As I walked past him and made my way to the second set of doors, I heard the voice of Jesus say, *He loves bananas.*

My internal reaction was simply, *Okay*, and I immediately headed to the produce department to pick up a few bananas for the man.

He probably needs some protein. Maybe I should get him something else to put in his backpack for later. I didn't question whether it was God's voice telling me to do this.

I just picked up a few more items that would be easily stored in his backpack and would not spoil.

I Said No

Although I had clearly heard the voice of Jesus telling me that the man loved bananas, the mother and cook in me begin to think, *That is just not enough. I am going to go over to the deli and pick up some warm fried chicken.*

Again, the voice of Jesus said, *I did not ask you to get him fried chicken.*

I am sure the look on my face was not pretty! It was likely a look of confusion, perhaps even a grimace. I do not like to be told no. Who does? I was helping this man!

I picked out the gift cards I had come to get and was walking toward the register when that gnawing thought came once again: *But I want to go get him some fried chicken. It is cold outside, and I just want to put some warm food in his belly.*

Again came the gentle voice of Jesus. *I did not ask you to get him chicken.*

Was Jesus saying no to me helping someone? I had never expected that! But He clearly had, and more than once. Still, I was wrestling with the thought. *I* felt the need to put something warm in his belly.

God did not tell me to do it. That was the issue. I was entertaining my own thoughts, wants, and wishes for this man. Why was I being told no to what I thought were perfectly reasonable actions? I couldn't understand it.

At the checkout, I paid for my items and went to deliver the bananas and other little food items to the homeless man. I still felt confused about why I couldn't buy the fried chicken. As I exited the first door, I made eye contact and greeted the man with a smile and asked, "You trying to keep warm, buddy?"

The man barely looked up at me but replied, "Yes, ma'am."

I extended my little bag of goodies to him and said, "May God bless you. Merry Christmas."

He reached his weather-worn hand out and gently took the bag.

As I began to walk away, another voice spoke up from behind me. A lady said, "Well, today must be your lucky day."

I turned to watch as the man looked up at her and tilted his head.

"You see," the woman continued, "I got you some fried chicken. It's still warm, and there are some napkins in there for you too."

My heart nearly leaped out of my chest! Hot tears instantly streamed down my cold cheeks as the sudden realization hit me: I was standing in the presence of my Jesus. Had He spoken to this woman the same way He had spoken to me?

It Was Just Bananas

I rushed to the car. After I pulled the door closed, I let the tears—which came from the deepest parts of me—stream down my face. Part of me wanted to get back out and rush back to the woman I did not know, grab her by the shoulders, spin her around, and scream, "Do you know what just happened? I mean, seriously, do you really know what just happened?"

But then I thought, *She'll see my tear-stained cheeks, think I've lost my mind, and wonder what on earth I am screaming about.* So instead, I sat and cried, and then I began praising God.

A few minutes later, I took my phone out, thinking, *I'll just tell my friends about this encounter with Christ. They have to know just exactly how real He is!*

I opened my Facebook account and saw the little prompt asking, "What's on your mind, Tammy?"

Well, Facebook, let me just tell you.

I began typing the incident out, pausing to wipe away the tears before continuing. I wrote a bit, wiped some more tears, and continued writing. Then I went back and reread the entire post and fixed all the typos. Just as I went to hit send, without any warning, the entire message was gone.

For the second time in just a few short minutes, I heard the voice of Jesus. This time He said, *No, not today. Today you go live.*

What?

Never having gone live on Facebook, I wasn't even sure how to do it, but I had to get this story out to my friends. And, of course, I wanted to obey. I wanted everyone to know how real Jesus is, how He is always with us at every moment. I sat in my car with tears still rolling down my cheeks and figured out how to go live. Then I told the story of a homeless man, me, some bananas, and a lady with fried chicken, the tears still streaming down my face.

That's the message millions saw December 14, 2016.

The next twenty-four hours were a blur. God began using this simple situation to speak to millions through the Facebook Live video. And people were responding! One year later, this video had been viewed over 100 million times, and people were still sending me messages.

But just six days after the video went viral, I stood in the shower at my momma's house in Florida asking God, "What are you doing here?" I mean, seriously, it was just bananas, and things seem to have gone—just bananas! Why was this simple act getting so much attention?

As I stood with the warm water running over my face, I said, "God, you have to be up to something. I simply responded to what you told me. I bought bananas, and then I heeded your words when you told me not to buy the fried chicken. This simple act is not worthy of such a massive outpouring from people. You must have something more in store. What are you trying to tell me, Lord? What are you trying to show me? How will you use this story to speak to so many others? What is it that you are trying to say to me—to us—that we are not hearing or understanding?"

Attention, Please

God often speaks to me in the most inopportune situations and times, because He then has my attention. In the shower, I can't run and hide from what He is trying to talk to me about. As I stood there in my momma's shower, with a head full of shampoo suds and my eyes closed tight, God gave me a vision.

I saw a little boy, perhaps about third-grade age, who had been chosen to sing the big solo in the Christmas pageant at school. I could see him waiting his turn with his teacher in the wing of the auditorium. As he stood there looking to the right, he saw his classmates singing their little hearts out. They performed all the proper motions to match the songs. Then he looked to the left toward the audience, and he saw the parents clapping, smiling, and snapping pictures of their favorite little performer. Then glancing back to the stage, he watched as his friends performed the tasks they had been given. One was the star shining bright, another, the tree standing tall and straight; others played the roles of the animals gathering around a makeshift manger where third graders, acting as Mary and Joseph, sat.

Suddenly, the stage went dark, and a single, bright spotlight took center stage. The teacher put her hands on the shoulders of the little boy waiting in the wings, leaned down, and whispered in his ear, "Okay, buddy, it's your turn. Go on out there!"

He stood, seemingly paralyzed. He looked back at his teacher and muttered, "Uh-uh, I can't go out there."

"Come on, buddy; you got this," she said. "We have practiced and rehearsed it. You got this!"

Frozen in fear, he shook his head and stuttered, "Uh, I can't do this. I . . . I can't go out there."

His teacher once again affirmed him, reminding him of the countless hours they'd worked together to commit the song to memory that he had so effortlessly sung in rehearsal. But he still stood there, trembling, completely overcome by fear, and violently shaking his head no and saying, "There is no way I can go out there."

Again, she took him by the shoulders, bent down, looked him square in the eyes, and for the final time, she said to him, "You got this!" Without warning, she thrust him out onto the stage, right in the middle of the spotlight, and there he stood.

There in the shower when I was soaking and wet and unable to run, God began to speak to me.

Now that I have thrown you out into the spotlight, you will either choose to do what I have created and called you to do, or you will choose to turn your back and walk away, and you will never come back to me. What will the choice be, my child?

Talk about getting my attention. I was finally ready to listen and, more importantly, to obey.

As my tears pouring down my face mingled with the water from the shower, I stretched out my hands in praise. "Yes, Lord, I will go, and I will do whatever you are asking of me. I will stop running from this calling and allow you to guide me in the direction you would have me to go."

I had known for years what that calling was, but I never felt worthy of such a calling. I always felt like, *Who am I, Lord?*

Who Am I, Lord?

For years, I had ignored this calling on my life. I should have won awards for the speed with which I ran in the opposite direction!

My calling is to speak and to write, to offer encouragement to those who feel broken and as if they are damaged goods.

My answer to God's call had always been, "Who am I, Lord? What makes you think anyone would ever listen to anything I have to say or to offer?"

At times in my life, I teetered on the edge of accepting that call, and then the enemy would swoop in. Before I knew it, I would take on that feeling of worthlessness once again and back away.

Perhaps you too have been there. Perhaps there is something you have felt God ask of you, and yet you have not stepped out in faith to answer that call.

What is He is asking of you today? Will you surrender to His call?

The Scripture that always comes to mind during times like this is Proverbs 3:5–6 (NKJV). "Trust in the Lord with all your heart and lean not on your own understanding; in all your ways, acknowledge Him, and He shall direct your path." I have recited this Scripture more times than I can count but often out of head knowledge, not heart knowledge. There is a huge difference between the two.

Perhaps you are reading this and feel a little nudge in your gut. Are you wondering, questioning even, "Is this God urging me to act?" You may be scared, and you don't want to look foolish if it turns out not to be Him tugging at your heart.

We'll be looking in the chapters ahead at how to have a better understanding of just how our Father speaks to us, how He gets our attention. It is not always a booming and thunderous voice from heaven, but it is all too often just a faint whisper. Sometimes it is not even directly to us but through a messenger He sends to us. Sometimes it is a confirmation delivered as we hide His Word in our hearts.

What has God placed on your heart to do? Have you begun or completed the task? Are you still running from it like I was? I urge you, don't make God create a spotlight moment to get your attention.

Proverbs 19:21 tells us, "Many are the plans of a person's heart, but it is the Lord's purpose that prevails." I encourage you to lay aside your fears of inadequacy and allow God's purpose to prevail in your life. God has been preparing you your entire life to fulfill your destiny in Him.

You may not understand it, but I assure you, you are far readier than you realize. Put your trembling hand in His and have faith that whatever it is, He will see you through it to completion.

FAINT WHISPERS

It helps to remember that according to God's Word in John 15:16, He chose you to complete the task He has called you to. We are not here by happenstance. We are here because God chose us!

When I really think about that, it blows my mind. Out of all the other people on this whole planet, God chose *me*. And He chose *you* too.

How Do You Know?

I have been asked repeatedly, "How did you know it was Jesus speaking to you?" Well, I just knew.

Have you ever been in a setting where you and your child were separated from one another? You set about looking for her among the throng of people, and suddenly you heard that cry of distress, "Mom?" You could be in a room of a hundred kids all screaming for their mothers, but you know and recognize your child's voice among all the rest.

You can recognize your child's voice because you are the momma, and you know your child. You know that fevered pitch her voice reaches when she is scared. You even know the difference between her various cries at night. After you put your child to bed, and you're sitting in the living room, relaxing, if you hear a cry from down the hall, you take a moment and analyze the cry. Is it an I'm-scared-of-the-dark cry or an I-need-a-drink-of-water cry? Perhaps it is an I'm-in-pain cry. Whatever the cry, you typically know the need before you even enter the bedroom. How? Because you know your child; you have

24

spent so much time with her that you know the meaning of the very sounds she utters.

That is exactly how it is with me and Jesus. I have spent so much time hiding His Word in my heart, praying to Him, and allowing Him to speak to me, that our relationship has reached a level of intimacy and trust. When He speaks to me, I just know. He longs to be that intimate with all His children, and that means you too.

Chosen

God has chosen us just as He chose David on the day he was called in from the field while tending his sheep. In 1 Samuel 16:10–13, we read how the prophet Samuel had checked out David's seven brothers then asked, "Is there anyone else?" Jesse, David's father, said, "Yes, there is. He is the youngest, and he is out in the field tending the flock."

As soon as David came in, God spoke to Samuel and told him: "Rise and anoint him; this is the one." Samuel then took a horn of oil and anointed David, and "from that day, the Spirit of the Lord came powerfully upon David."

I believe that in the same way God chose and anointed David, He will anoint His chosen here on earth today. We, as a body of believers, need only to position ourselves to be used of God, to be anointed for His purpose. So let's lift one another up in prayer and urge each other on in the journey toward heaven.

Favorites

I have been getting acquainted via the internet with the stories of a man named Ray Carmen, who is a shepherd and posts on Facebook as "Enjoy the Shepherd." He tells of traveling to another state to speak to a youth camp about the heart of a shepherd. After receiving a huge welcome, he said it was obvious that the teens had studied him and his flock in preparation for the event.

Ray asked them, "What is a shepherd?" and "What are the names of some of my sheep?" When he asked, "Which one of my sheep do I love the most?" the answer, of course, was, "All of them."

The Bible says we're like sheep. Just as a shepherd loves his sheep, God loves us all but uses those who trust the Shepherd with all their hearts.

When God chose David to be the king to lead his people, He did not pick the strongest, the best looking, or even the smartest man. God wasn't looking for a leader who people considered wise or overly attractive. God looked at the heart of the would-be king. He wanted a heart that trusted Him fully, one that would follow Him no matter where He led.

I want to be one who trusts God with all my heart.

The day I bought the bananas, I was trusting my Good Shepherd and His instructions to me, and it made all the difference.

Scripture Focus

> You did not choose me, but I chose you
> and appointed you so that you might go

and bear fruit—fruit that will last—and so that whatever you ask in my name the Father will give you. (John 15:16)

Guide me in your truth and teach me, for you are God my Savior, and my hope is in you all day long. (Psalm 25:5)

Trust in the Lord with all your heart and lean not on your own understanding; in all your ways submit to him, and he will make your paths straight. (Proverbs 3:5–6)

Challenge

I challenge you to simply whisper, "Yes, Lord."

Challenge Accepted

What do you feel God is asking you to do that you have not yet done?
Why have you not stepped out in faith and completed the task?
What steps will you take this week to fulfill God's request?

Will You Pray with Me?

Father God, today I surrender to your complete will for my life. Go before me and guide my steps so I can complete this task in a way that will bring honor and glory to you. In Jesus's name, amen.

TWO

GET IN THE GROOVE: CREATURES OF HABIT

Did you know the Bible compares us to sheep more than five hundred times? When I learned that, I was so intrigued I decided to learn more about the creatures with which we share many traits.

In a herd, when one sheep moves, they typically all follow, even if following is not a good idea. From birth, young lambs are taught to follow the older sheep. Once that habit is established, they simply carry on following the leader. They are definitely creatures of habit.

While raising his sheep, Ray Carman noticed how well they adapted to his pattern of life. He woke each morning at about the same time, got his day started, and headed out the door at nearly the same time every day to tend to the flock. One morning he was running a few minutes behind. He looked out the window and saw that all his sheep had gathered in the place where he would normally be at that time. Obviously, the sheep had no clocks to tell time by.

Ray got curious. Over the next few days he purposely waited a few minutes later than normal to get started in the morning. Every day, the sheep followed the pattern he'd set long before and were waiting for him when and where they'd expected him to be each morning.

Sheep are creatures who are most comfortable sticking to their habits.

I'd like to suggest you and I are too!

I read a story in BBC News that recounted how more than 450 sheep fell to their deaths in eastern Turkey following a leader that tried to cross a fifteen-meter-deep ravine. In total that day, more than 1,500 sheep made the jump off that cliff. Those that lived did so because they landed on the cushion created in the ravine by the first 450 sheep who plummeted to their deaths. Those that died did so because they were simply following along and going through the motions without wondering where such blind following might lead.

Where are you today?

We, like sheep, enjoy our routines, but routines can be harmful or helpful. Is your life structured to avoid the pitfall of bad habits or bad routines? Or have you allowed the structure of your life to be one of unquestioned routines to the point that you are just going through the motions and hoping for a good outcome without considering where your blind actions might lead?

A Trip to Juvie

As I began thinking about our need to maintain good habits and structure in our lives, I was reminded of a scene that played out in front of me a few years back.

I sat on my front porch enjoying a cold glass of sweet tea on one very hot summer night. The heat index of 106 degrees had finally subsided, and the skies were clear and beautiful. A neighbor was trimming her shrubs, another watering her flowers, and across the street some boys played on the baseball field, kicking up dust as they rounded the bases, heading for home plate.

Further down the sidewalk, a couple of young teens, a boy and a girl, walked hand in hand, trailed by an even younger girl who was focusing on the cell phone she was holding up to her face. As the trio came within earshot, I overheard the following conversation.

"Seriously?" the boy asked.

"Yeah, seriously," the girl next to him answered. "My friends who have been to juvie say they love it. They have so much fun there. One friend of mine got into trouble on purpose just so she could go back."

My gut reaction was, *What? You've got to be kidding me!* This was a bit of a shock-and-awe moment for me. I've been a guest speaker at our local juvenile detention center on multiple occasions. I knew, as a rule, what goes on in that facility. I even knew many of the children lodged there due to my many years of service in a children's ministry that serves what society calls "at-risk youth."

I sat there on my front porch doing some serious thinking about what those kids had said. I wondered what we were teaching these children if juvie is a bowl of cherries, or a cakewalk, or at the very least, someplace they were willing to reoffend to returned to?

Really? Had they enjoyed their time there? I found that difficult to believe. My next thought was, *Yeah right. They just said that because they wanted to act all big and bad when really, they were probably scared out of their wits the whole time.*

But then I thought a little harder about the kids I had known who had been in juvie—really thought about what a lot of those kids were missing in their lives at home.

And I knew. They really did prefer being there.

Imagine a fifteen-year-old in trouble because she is labeled incorrigible. Let's say she's been staying out all hours of the night and day, skipping school, and often not coming home for two or three days at a time. This same teen has already been picked up by police at an underage party, intoxicated to the point of being legally drunk. Released to the custody of her parents, she is free to leave and be gone another three days before finally coming home to sleep it off. No one noticed or cared or prevented her from leaving again and again.

When I think of this child and her family, I see a family trapped in a downward spiral of dysfunction, chaos, and mayhem. It's a pattern, a lifestyle that has become normal to them. The young one, after all, is only following the leader in many cases. Granted, this may not always be the case, but often it is.

Many children in juvie are being brought up in homes where drugs and alcohol are parental issues. Abuse is common, expected, and tolerated. It has become a generational habit that no one questions or sees. Family trees are full of unfulfilled dreams, hopes, and wishes that have faded with every change of season. Generations have resigned themselves to settling if they even recognize what is happening.

I believe that some of them do recognize what is happening. This child, this seemingly rebellious teenager, when you really look deep inside, is using her actions to scream, "I deserve better! I want more out of this life!" This scared child, this baby, really, is screaming to find a better way, a life where she can dream and hope and wish and break cycles to accomplish what generations before her were not able to accomplish.

In juvie, the child is given uniform clothing to wear and told when to shower, when to go to class, when to go let off steam in the gym, when to eat, when to study, when to do this, and when to do that. This is called structure. It's a routine! Imagine that! The very thing this child believed she was fighting against is really what she craved all along, deep within. Structure.

Isn't that just like us as believers? We rebel against being told what to do; we want our own ways; we say we want freedom. Year after year, we press on with unhealthy habits, many of which go unquestioned. Do we not also crave the structure that allows us to create good habits, habits that can sustain us in even the worst trials of life? We do.

Jesus knows that. He offers us structure of the very best kind. We can meet our Shepherd where He is, every day. He offers us the order and guidance He knows we need.

A Model Prayer

God knows His children need structure and routine. After all, that is how He created us. He knows we want to be heard, and He knows we want to hear from Him. We don't always know how to hear Him, though, or what to say back to Him, because our relationship with Him is unlike our other relationships.

This is why He gave us the perfect model of prayer in what is typically known as the Lord's Prayer. Matthew 6:9–13 (NKJV) shows us exactly how to pray; it gives us guidelines and helps us build a healthy habit to hear from and speak to our Lord.

> *Our Father in heaven*, hallowed be Your name, Your kingdom come, Your will be done, on earth as it is in heaven. Give us this day our daily bread. And forgive us our debts, as we forgive our debtors. And do not lead us into temptation but deliver us from the evil one. For Yours is the kingdom and the power and the glory forever. Amen.

This is God's template for prayer. Although we are welcome to repeat this prayer daily, it is not intended to be one we recite by rote, but rather to be used as a guide to systematically align our priorities with those of our Father's.

I'll do my best to break this prayer down and show you how we need to position ourselves in prayer today so we can hear the voice of God.

"Our Father in heaven."

God is our Father, and He is seated in heaven. As we pray this, we are acknowledging who He is and our position as members of the family of God. As you pray, acknowledge who He is and where He is seated in your own words, and acknowledge your position as His child.

"Hallowed be Your name."

According to the *Merriam-Webster Dictionary*, *hallowed* means "holy, consecrated, or sacred." When we pray this, we say, "Holy and sacred is your name, God." Using your own words, tell God that you give reverence to who He is.

"Your kingdom come, Your will be done."

When we look around the world, we see all sorts of reasons to ask God to come quickly, to sound that trumpet and call us home so the many hurting people in this world, you and I included, will be set free from pain. But while we await that glorious return, we trust that His will is perfect for our lives, and we ask Him to bring His will to completion in us every day.

"Give us this day our daily bread."

We only need to trust God to supply our every need for today and today only. That means we depend on Him to provide every day. That dependence keeps us close. We are not asking just for physical bread but for everything we need, even the very breath of life. Trusting God to meet our needs daily shows our complete trust and dependence on Him.

"And forgive us our debts, as we forgive our debtors."

This is a very hard truth for most of us to understand, but we will not see the kingdom of heaven if we refuse to forgive. Colossians 3:13 tells us, "If anyone has a complaint against another, even as Christ forgave you, so you also must do." This is so important to Christ that He wants us to keep this attitude of forgiveness front and center in our daily prayer life.

I get it; forgiveness can be so hard. I believe when we forgive as we have been forgiven, it is like cleaning out a badly clogged drain. Suddenly, the clog breaks free, and the water, the *living water* in this case, can freely flow! God longs to speak to us, to comfort us, to love us, but we have the ultimate responsibility of keeping the channel of communication unclogged.

"And do not lead us into temptation but deliver us from the evil one."

Temptation is often described as a trial or a test. When we pray this, we are saying something like, "God, I am asking you to keep me from this trial, this test. But if you chose to allow it to come my way, I pray you would deliver me, protect me, keep me from the Evil One, the Enemy, who is trying to lure me away from you. I need your strength to endure and conquer this temptation."

This model prayer, the Lord's Prayer, shows us how to approach our Father in heaven every day. We acknowledge and give reverence to who He is to us. Then we pray for and ask that His will be perfected in and through those things that grieve us to the point of us anxiously awaiting His return. Next, we bring our requests before Him, trusting Him to supply our every need for this day only. This is so we must return to Him as a daily habit. Then, we search our hearts and ask forgiveness for anything that may stand in the way of our communication with Him. We also forgive those who we may feel have hurt or wronged us. Finally, we ask Him to protect us from or in a trial or test we're experiencing. We acknowledge our trust in Him to guard our hearts against the Enemy who seeks to devour us.

Taking a quick self-examination, how would you say your daily prayers line up with the model prayer God gave us as a guide? Are you making the most of each day, each prayer? Is your prayer life one that is intimate and attentive?

Remember those sheep that were killed by blindly following what others were doing? We do our own cliff diving when we routinely follow along with what others are doing or what we have always done, sometimes to our great harm.

When you examine your prayer life, do you find you are repeating the same praises and prayers every time? If so, dig a little deeper and ask yourself this question: Am I praying with my head, a "normal" prayer, one that has become routine? If so, remember when you pray with your head, saying what you always say, you do so out of knowledge, not faith. This type of prayer is one of just going through the motions. It may very well lead you over a cliff because you are not truly paying attention.

But if you find that you are you praying from your heart, a prayer that is full of love, respect, fresh self-examination, repentance, and mindful purpose, then you will be praying with a heart of expectation. You can trust that you are honoring God by following the example He set for us.

Morning Routine

If you're wondering how your prayer life lines up, a quick look at your morning routine will most likely provide the answer.

Imagine it's six in the morning, and your alarm goes off to signal the start of a grand new day. You jump up and grab a quick shower. You dry off and then throw your hair up in a towel before heading in to the wake the kids. You step over the junk all over the floor, trying to avoid a small disaster, and you tap the kid in the bottom bunk on the foot and the kid in the top bunk on the shoulder. "Come on guys; you don't want to be late."

Next, you rush to the kitchen and toss some breakfast on the table before getting ready for your workday. Once you have thrown together the perfect outfit for the big meeting, you check on the kids to usher them along. You toss a roast in the crockpot for dinner and finish preparing the kids' lunches just as the bus rounds the corner. You hand each child a somewhat nutritious lunch, kiss them goodbye as they run for the bus, and grab your keys as you head to the car.

This is the start of the day for many of you reading this. I can almost see you grinning and nodding in agreement. I know, because this has been my life too! We are creatures of habit. Just like the juvie kids knew in their hearts, we like when things are in order. We are so used to our routines that we can do them with our eyes closed or seemingly in our sleep. We're like sheep waiting for their shepherd each morning, even if he seems to be late.

Sometimes this is good; great habits tend to bring great results. However, sometimes we can become so comfortable in our routine that we are simply going through the motions. We must be very careful to guard against those types of routines and habits that threaten to steal our time from our Father. We must make time to build our relationship with Christ and protect that time.

I have found that oh-dark-thirty (pre-dawn) is the best time for me to meet with my Father. Why? Because nobody *needs* me at that time of the morning. It is *my* time, and it is sacred. What better way to start my day than at the feet of Jesus. When we meet with Him regularly, we build intimacy. By doing that, we begin to learn and understand the many ways He speaks to us, and we will learn to discern His voice quickly.

That Faint Whisper

I love that He loves us so very much that when we come to Him in prayer, the most important thing is that we have a clear channel of communication with Him. To clear that line of communication, we must make sure that we have repented and that nothing is hindering us from hearing His voice—that we have unclogged that drain, so to speak, and our voices can reach Him, and His reach us.

Through the structure of the Lord's Prayer and creating a routine, a habit of purposeful prayer, we will begin to break down the walls of silence. If we seek Him, we will find Him and hear His voice in our lives.

If we fail to clear that line of communication, if we fail to let God do a work in us first, then we will fail to hear from Him. We will not be living the abundant life He intended for us to live. With our line of communication clear, we will learn how to hear those faint whispers.

Come to Me

Remember how the sheep adapted to the shepherd's morning routine?

It is the same with our walk with Jesus. Just like the sheep would wait for shepherd Ray at their normal place to gather, we should consistently come to the place where our Father feeds us. And, like the flock, we should wait in great anticipation for our Shepherd to come and to meet with us, right where we are.

You will find in your journey that sometimes that place is in your "prayer closet" at home. Sometimes that place is with a body of like-minded believers, like we will discuss in the next chapter. It might be in your car at lunch hour or any number of other places you and God can meet. Regardless of where it is, the important thing is to make it a habit to meet with Him. We must speak to Him as He has modeled for us. We must have our channel of communication with God clear of all debris. And then we can clearly hear His voice.

Scripture Focus

> Search me, oh God, and know my heart; test me and know my anxious thoughts. See if there is any offensive way in me and lead me in the way everlasting. (Psalm 139:23–24)

> The thief comes only to steal and kill and destroy. I came that they may have life and have it abundantly. (John 10:10 esv)

Challenge

I challenge you to be consistent in your prayer life. Follow the example we were given in the Lord's Prayer. First give respect to who He is and lavish Him with your praise, worship, and complete adoration, because this is what He deserves. Ask Him to search your heart. Take time to pause and listen for His revelation to you. We must not rush through this; He longs to spend time with you. He really loves you that much!

Challenge Accepted

In examining your prayer habits, do you see any changes that need to be made?

If so, what steps will you take to make these changes?

Will You Pray with Me?

Father in heaven, you are worthy to be praised! You are sovereign, you are holy, and you are just. Father, as I wholly depend on you, I ask that you supply all my needs today, physically and spiritually. Help me forgive those who have caused me hurt and pain, just as you have forgiven me of my sins.

Your word is a lamp unto my feet and a light unto my path. Keep me from the Evil One who seeks to destroy me. If you choose to allow such a test or trial, I pray you would order each step I take and deliver me from his grasp. I give praise to you alone, for you are worthy. Amen.

THREE

STRENGTH IN NUMBERS:
EVEN THE BARNYARD UNDERSTANDS

Shepherd Ray has lived in rural areas most of his life and has observed the behavior of the animals on the farm. At certain times of the year, he has noticed many different types of animals gathered together in one field. He's seen sheep, cows, chickens, horses, dogs, and every so often, a cat or two. That is a lot of different types of animals in one place at one time. The amazing thing is, each of them provides a benefit for the other. They are better together.

The chickens, for example, peck around and eat ticks and bugs that could pester the sheep. Almost as if they are thankful, the sheep stir up more insects for those chickens to eat as they walk around the paddock. A guardian dog roams around the perimeter, providing protection against wily coyotes and other predators seeking to devour the livestock. The animals provide a family and a job for the guard dog. The horse provides a sense of dignity and stability to all the creatures and transportation for the master. Each animal is different, but also, they each play a significant role in their "family." In nature it seems there is a reason for everything.

Have you ever noticed how the cattle and the sheep gather in one big group and hunker down together just before a big storm arrives? They know there is strength in numbers, and they are more likely to survive the storm if they weather it *together*.

If we will look closely enough, we may just learn something. There is a reason for all of us in the family of God with our varied talents and roles.

Maybe you know someone whom, if you've asked, "Have you been to church?" always comes back with, "I don't have to go to church to be a Christian! I can sit right here in my pajamas and watch any television preacher I want today and be just fine."

Sound familiar? Maybe it's your friend. Maybe it's you. Sometimes, it is tempting even to me. But, like the animals, we can't be safe—or useful—if we go it alone.

We Need Each Other

When the pastor took to the pulpit on a Wednesday night, I could tell by just looking that there was a struggle going on within him. His burdened heart caused tears to stream down his cheeks. When he began to speak, his voice audibly shook. His message, though, was very clear as he told us how much we need one another.

That week had been very difficult for his church. It seemed every time he turned around, the prayer chain had been initiated. The requests coming through were all serious in nature. One person had a blood clot in a femoral artery. A man needed a miracle as his liver and kidneys were shutting down. A woman requested intercession for a breast biopsy. There was a colon cancer diagnosis. Prayer was requested for the victims of a head-on collision between a car and a semi and for small children testing positive for the flu. In fact, that season, eighty-four children had already lost their lives nationwide due to the flu epidemic.

The pastor's heart broke for these families in great need, but as he looked out that Wednesday, his heart also broke for those missing from the pews, which were not as full as they usually were. I could see that his heart grieved. The minister longed for his congregation to gather together in Jesus's name and cry out to our Father in heaven and intercede on behalf of all these families.

He spoke to those in attendance, explaining in detail Hebrews 10:23–25.

> Let us hold unswervingly to the hope we profess, for he who promised is faithful. And let us consider how we may spur one another on toward love and good deeds, not giving up meeting together, as some are in the habit of doing, but encouraging one another—and all the more as you see the Day approaching.

From the platform, with tears pouring down his face, he reminded the congregation to not forsake meeting together, especially in times of trouble. He said, in times like that we, as a body of believers, need to come together to strengthen our bonds, pray for one another, and to use our gifts to protect and encourage one another. His heart was burdened for his church, because he understood the great need for the church to gather and weather the storms of life together.

I am sure you have heard this before, but I will say it again: God uses ordinary people to do extraordinary things.

I don't know about you, but I am very ordinary. I still cry out to God, "Use me, Lord." And He does! If I choose to give up meeting together and stay at home in my pretty pajamas by myself and only watch my favorite TV preacher, how will you, my sister or brother in Christ, reach out to me in your time of great need? How will I hear you? See you? Hug and protect you?

Who will I call on when the storm hits my own house? No one will gather around me to protect me.

When I'm reminded of the importance of assembling in God's house, I think of Matthew 18:20, "For where two or three gather in my name, there I am with them." What a beautiful promise! He will be there when we are; that alone makes us better together.

The next time you are in church, take a good look around. As you sit in the service and glance at those that fill the pews each week, take a mental picture of who you see. You'll find a wide assortment of individuals with varying educations, bank account balances, marital statuses, numbers of children, and most importantly, personal testimonies.

The people who sit in church near me are ordinary like me. We are all so ordinary that we represent people who are just like us in almost every church, every workplace, on every block, and in every town. We come from all walks of life when we enter God's house; after all, the church is a hospital for the hurt and the broken, right? But when we come together as one to worship our Father in heaven, all our differences fade away. We each find our place as a child of the King, together, side by side, with our sisters and brothers. God wants to use all this diversity, His diversity, to teach, to admonish, and to speak into all of us.

What gifts does God want to lavish on you, so you can be an active part of building His kingdom? Perhaps you will be the one He chooses to give the gift of spiritual wisdom or spiritual discernment. Perhaps your hands will be anointed with the gift of healing or your tongue with the gift of prophecy. Each gift is a gift from God not to be used for personal gain but for the building and edification of the body of Christ. We use those gifts to speak for Him to others.

As I looked around my own congregation, I began to praise God that He has assembled us together. Together we can bring Hebrews 10 to life. We can pray for and encourage one another and spur our brothers and sisters on.

To be the best encourager I can be, something I have always done is to fix a big Sunday dinner. While preparing the meal, I pray about the one needing encouragement *that day*. When God reveals to me who that person or family is, I invite them to take a seat at our table.

While we dine on pot roast, fresh bread, and the occasional tomato soup cake, we have an opportunity to share our struggles and offer words of encouragement. After eating, we gather in the living room and pray together before they head home with full bellies and encouraged hearts. None of this would be possible if I remained behind closed doors on Sundays, listening to a televangelist.

I do know that sometimes, due to illness or transportation issues, watching televised teaching is a person's only option. If that is true for a season, I know God will most definitely meet you where you are. But if you are able to get out and surround yourself with like-minded believers, even if only once per week, you'll find the strength that comes from being in fellowship.

If you bring your burdens into the house of God and you begin to open up and share those burdens with one another, God will honor that, and He will speak and move in ways that our minds cannot conceive. There *is* strength in numbers. We *are* better together.

Eyes to See and Ears to Hear

Now that the line of communication has been unclogged, you can walk into your worship service at church with a new attitude. Queue the music of the great Patti LaBelle and her song about having a new attitude. You see, once you get everything out of the way that was hindering your communication with Him, you will find a new level of freedom in your worship. You will see and hear God in ways you may have never known before. Unclogging that line is like opening blind eyes and deaf ears; it all becomes so much clearer.

Let's say you have been praying about something very private, very personal, something that you are asking God to move on quickly. The worship leader takes the center platform, and the lyrics come up on the screen. As you begin singing, the words of the song hit you like a ton of bricks! Tears begin to fall as you realize all that you have crying out to God about is already in the palm of His hand. You just needed to be reminded that He's got you covered. The lyrics did that. God used the lyrics to say, "It's okay, my child. I am already at work in that situation." God speaks through music when we worship together.

Perhaps you're in a service and a spontaneous "popcorn testimony" session breaks out. For those not familiar with this, it's where one person stands to offer a personal testimony or a word of praise, and then, one after another, they just keep popping up. That last person stands up and shares a triumphant testimony about God working out the details of a situation that may be the very same situation you are just then going through. God uses that testimony to speak life to your situation. He reminds you, *See, I took care of that one, and I will take care of you too.* God speaks through the testimony of others when we gather together to share and to listen.

Perhaps you spent your last ten dollars on gas just to get to church, and it is another week until payday. At the close of the service, someone comes to you, shakes your hand, and slips you a twenty saying, "It was great to see you today. I'll be praying for you this week." The cash is not spoken of. It is simply there. God saw your commitment and your sacrifice to be in church. He honored that by speaking to that individual and asking him or her to bless you. This was God speaking to you and saying, *Thank you for trusting me with your last ten dollars.* God speaks through the actions of others.

None of this would have happened if you had stayed home. It also may not have happened if you are attending a church that just doesn't feel right or if you are not actively participating in church activities and creating personal connections. Go! Ask God to keep your eyes peeled to *see* the ways He is speaking and your ears open to *hear* the ways He is speaking to you.

Shelter in the Storm

Remember the barnyard and all the animals I talked about, each one with a different purpose in the animal family? What is your role in the family of God? What purpose are you serving during the storm today? Maybe this is a time of need for you, and you are in the middle of the huddle, trusting those around you to protect you, encourage you, and lift you up in prayer during the storm. If you're facing the storm alone, why are you?

You need to be in that huddle to hear God speaking to you through others. Are you a sheep that is about to succumb to the antics of the wily coyote because the guard dog falls asleep on the job? A guard is one who surrounds a brother or sister in need, fervently praying for him or her and speaking for and over him or her. Your guard dog can't shout warnings to you, another way the Lord may speak to you, if you are not in a place where you're near each other.

Maybe you don't even have a guard dog looking out for you; you're not in church at all. You are completely on your own. That is a dangerous place to be. When we try to go it alone and give up meeting together, we open ourselves up to the possibility of defeat. Without sharing those precious times of fellowship where we build friendships on faith and trust, we can be easily distracted and become vulnerable to the enemy's attacks.

Are you hiding behind a mask with a beautiful smile that says I have the tiger by the tail, while in reality, the tiger is about to take the very last bite from you and render you dead? This is not what God intended for you! He loves you and wants to surround you with people who will love you and lift you up in prayer.

We cannot begin to hear the voice of God in our lives when we fail to allow Him to create and build relationships with those He wants to use *in* our lives, as well as us in theirs. We hear Him through their voices; they hear Him through ours. We cannot put on a mask and an I've-got-this-all-by-myself attitude. Hebrews 10:24–25 says, "And let us consider how we may spur one another on toward love and good deeds, not giving up meeting together, as some are in the habit of doing, but encouraging one another—and all the more as you see the Day approaching."

Often, God uses other people to deliver a message to us. Incredibly, God uses ordinary people just like you and me to speak life into others. That word we speak on God's behalf may be the difference in them giving up or pressing forward. It may be an issue of life or death.

You need to be within speaking, nudging, or barking distance so God can use someone to speak to you on His behalf too!

If we fail to build relationships in the church, we may be left standing alone during the greatest storms of life. What a blessing it is to know my brothers and sisters in Christ are lifting me in prayer when I am too broken to lift my own voice to Him. God not only speaks through them to me, but they also speak for me to Him.

He Sent a Prophet

When you hear the words *prophecy* or *prophet*, what do think of? For me, old television shows and movies, perhaps an episode of *Little House on the Prairie*, come to mind. I think of a large preacher man with a booming voice holding service under a big tent in the heat of summer.

While this picture is not quite accurate, it is not too far from the days of old. The prophet may or may not "boom," and we are more likely sitting in a brick-and-mortar building with the air set on a cool seventy-two degrees.

When word gets out that a minister with the gift of prophecy is coming to speak, the service will be packed with standing room only. Why? It could be for one of two reasons. Some will come because they are curious, and they have never witnessed this spiritual gift in person.

Others will come because they want to receive a message from the prophet. Those seeking a message either trust the prophet or want to test the prophet to see if he "has the goods," so to speak.

What exactly is this gift of prophecy? I am just learning about this gift, so my knowledge of this subject is limited. In my studies, I found 2 Peter 1:21 that says, "For prophecy never had its origin in the human will, but prophets, though human, spoke from God as they were carried along by the Holy Spirit." My interpretation of this verse is this: God has a message to deliver, and He is going to use a *chosen* human as His delivery method.

Imagine getting an envelope in the mail and inside you find a handwritten note signed, "Love, God." The message was from God, but it was delivered to you in an envelope. That envelope represents the prophet—the method of delivery. This is just another example how God uses ordinary people to do extraordinary things to build His church.

You will notice above that I italicized the word *chosen* in talking about God's delivery method. I can't just wake up tomorrow and say, "Well that sounds like fun. I think I want to be God's delivery man." You cannot just *choose* to be a prophet. God calls you, and He gifts you. There is no college degree that you can *earn* to be a prophet.

It is important to note that God cannot contradict Scripture, as God does not contradict Himself. But remember this world is full of *false prophets*, so we must be wise.

I was saved—became a Christian—in the first church I went to. I spent many wonderful years there. Having not been raised in the church, I soaked up all the teaching. I was thirsty for the Jesus I had just had a saving encounter with. That church did not teach or talk about the gift of prophecy, so I had never encountered this in the twenty-plus years of my journey.

Looking back, I now understand that prophecy is one of those things we sometimes just ignore in the church. I think we often take on an attitude of, "If I don't acknowledge it, I won't have to try and understand it." Maybe we think it's something God has stopped using after the Old Testament prophets or the death of the apostles. That is not true. If God really wants to get your attention, He may very well use one of those "ignored" gifts to speak to us and teach us.

We hear God through other believers in the huddle who have that gift of prophecy.

In July of 2016, just six months before my viral video, I attended a special service where someone with the gift of prophecy was speaking. I had no background, no teaching on the gift of prophecy, and really did not even know what to think about it. I was incredibly naïve about the subject. I had been told before walking into the service that this man had the gift of prophecy. "If he prophecies over you, you can pretty much take it to the bank," my friend told me. Well, me being me, in my unbelief, I just had one of those nod-and-grin moments. Have you been guilty of this gesture as well? I was skeptical.

After the man had delivered his message, he asked me to stand up right there in front of everyone. We were from out of town and among strangers, and I was being asked to stand up. I was not going to be disrespectful in God's house, so I stood. The man began to speak over me. All I remember is him repeatedly saying, "God is going to give you a word, and you are going to speak to the nations. Get ready; it is going to happen *fast*. Get ready!"

I learned in moments like this, someone accompanying you needs to write it down or to hit Record on a handy-dandy cell phone for later recollection. When a true prophet of God delivers a message, you will be so struck that you are not likely to remember anything but the highlights. You will want to remember, as it's God speaking to you through others.

As my husband and I left the service, we looked at each other, and I said, "What was that all about?" In my unbelief, I laughed like a schoolgirl all the way to the car. "He said I was going to speak to nations." I laughed again and said, "Yeah, right. Who am I that God would have me speak to nations?"

Insert even more side-splitting laughter here.

Fast-forward to December 14, 2016, when the prophecy would prove true.

God put a word in my mouth. By His will, I spoke that word to the nations. That word, through the video and now through this book, is still speaking to nations! I am no longer a Doubting Thomas! There are those among us who have the gift of prophecy. God made me a believer when He brought this to pass. God used that man to speak to me, to prepare me.

The next time, there will be no laughter! I pray that if God chooses to use a prophet to speak to me again, it causes me to rise, square my shoulders, and adjust my armor while trusting and moving forward into the fulfillment of the prophecy.

God used another believer, in an assembly of believers, to speak to me. If I hadn't been there, I would not have heard. If my brother, the prophet, would not have been there, I would not have heard. We both had to be in the service, so God could speak His will to us. Believe me—I heard it!

Be Intentional

Gathering together in church is up close and personal. I don't set aside the importance of social media. Look how God used it to send my video viral. It's probably how I've been introduced to many of you. But in this era of constant contact with social media and texting, we often get so wrapped up we fail to get personal with others. Or we make connections, but we fail to build them. Hebrews 10 shows this is not the example Christ would have us to follow. I am finding it necessary to be very intentional these days in building those one-on-one connections and relationships.

We have a choice. We can create virtual friendships, send them virtual hugs, and leave comments with little praying hands icons. (If you are not into social media, those hugs are a thing.) Or we can choose to step out from behind the screen and anonymity of social media and embrace and connect with those around us. But you will never know unless you step out. I encourage you to ask God to help you be more intentional in building Christ-centered, storm-weathering relationships. It is when we gather together that God can use us to help one another.

The Enemy would like you to think you have nothing to offer someone else. We must not be overcome by the lies of the Enemy but rather be intentional in the ways of moving forward in the kingdom. Grandmothers can mentor young mothers by sharing their years of experience and wisdom. Seasoned gentlemen can teach young boys everything from how to change the oil in the grocery-getter to teaching him the ways of being a chivalrous young man. Nearly all of us can offer a night of babysitting to a weary mom, cook a meal for someone who has been ill, or just sit and have coffee with someone who is confined to their home or nursing facility.

We all can offer to lay hands on each other as we pray. You see, we *do* all have something to offer. We just must be willing for God to use us. We also need to be willing to allow others to speak into our lives as much as we must allow God to use us to speak into the lives of those around us.

God may have those He wants to speak to using your journey or testimony. Are you aligning yourself or meeting with others to be used as a voice for God? And, just as importantly, are you gathering with others to receive a word from God through them?

Scripture Focus

> And let us consider how we may spur one another on toward love and good deeds, not giving up meeting together, as some are in the habit of doing, but encouraging one another—and all the more as you see the Day approaching. (Hebrews 10:24–25)

> Therefore encourage one another and build each other up, just as in fact you are doing. (1 Thessalonians 5:11)

> For where two or three gather in my name, there I am with them. (Matthew 18:20)

Challenge

I challenge you to make it a point to gather together with like-minded people so you can bear one another's burdens and so God can use the fellowship of other like-minded people to speak to you. He may just use you to speak to someone else.

Challenge Accepted

Where will you gather with other like-minded believers this week?

Name one person who you will reach out to and connect with this week.

This week send a note of encouragement to someone that you know is weathering a storm.

Will You Pray with Me?

Father God, may I never fail to praise you for who you are and all that you are! Forgive me for my unbelief and for asking, "Who am I that you would send me?" Strengthen and renew godly relationships in my life so we can weather the storms of this life together. Your Word says where two or more gather in your name, you are in the midst. Use me, and put me among those I can speak life into. Bring me into those relationships that will build us up and mutually encourage us as we journey toward the prize of heaven while hearing from you here on earth. Amen.

FOUR

WHAT'S IN YOUR TREASURE CHEST?

A treasure chest holds things that are important, things that are sentimental, things we never want to lose. Have you ever considered that your mind is like a treasure chest—a storehouse of so much information, so many memories?

The treasure chest of my memories would have a quilt my grandmother made for me and some of the favorite outfits my daughter wore when she was a baby. There would be a special gift my other grandmother gave me before her passing and all the special projects my daughter did while she was in school. These things bring memories to mind when we touch or see them.

Speaking of the information we store in our minds, I've told my daughter that if I ever make it on a trivia TV show, she would be my phone-a-friend contact. She has an uncanny knack for hiding obscure information in her mind. I just talked with her on the phone, and she shared with me how pineapples grow on bushes not trees. They do not ripen any more after they are picked; if not eaten, they will simply rot. She also told me if you turn the pineapple upside down for a day or so before cutting it, it will redistribute all the sweet nectar that has pooled at the bottom of the fruit from sitting that way too long.

Do you store information like this too?

The way God made our minds and our memories is so intriguing. Do you ever have those moments when a certain smell or a certain word or phrase transport you back to another time, another place?

I sometimes struggle to remember what I had for dinner last week, where I had it, or if I completed a specific task. But let me walk into an old barn, and the aroma instantly transports me to a memory back in 1975 of me standing in the old barn at my papa's. I love that smell, and I don't even know *what* the smell is. The memory takes me to a time when I was young and carefree and spending time with my childhood hero, my papa. It is almost a euphoric feeling, all created in my mind.

Buried Treasure

We are called to hide the Word of God in our hearts, to commit it to memory. That, too, is hiding treasure in the treasure chest of our hearts and minds. According to Ephesians 6:17, an integral part of the full armor of God is "the sword of the spirit, which is the word of God." Why is this important, and what does it have to do with hearing the voice of God? Psalm 119:11 says, "I have hidden your word in my heart that I might not sin against you." Hiding God's Word in our hearts will help to hold us to the standard God set before us.

The very first Scripture most of us committed to memory was John 3:16: "For God so loved the world that he gave his one and only Son, that whoever believes in him shall not perish but have eternal life." This is the one verse that many, even non-Christians, know by heart. This is an important verse that talks of Christ coming to save us and eternal life, but it is not the only Scripture we should have committed to memory.

We don't need to sit down and memorize the entire Bible. But we need to be reading the Word, so it can nourish us and dwell in us.

My daughter was active in Bible quizzing. She committed large portions of Scripture to memory during those days, to the point that if the quizmaster read a verse and altered a single word, she knew which word was changed and what the word should have been. She had, and still has, mad memory skills. This is great but not feasible for everyone and not what is really expected of us.

What is expected? A commitment to spend time in the Word. Why? Because God uses the words we have hidden in our hearts, words we may not even remember we have read, to speak to us. He loves to unearth these buried word treasures at just the right moments.

A Kiss from the King

To show how God speaks to us from the Scriptures at just the right time, I would like to introduce you to a couple of my social media followers and new friends.

One of them, Sally, stopped one day at a local convenience mart for a quick soda while she was on her mail route. There she noticed a mom and four small children gathered around the slushy machine. Sally thought about how hard it must be to be a mom of four in today's world as she watched the mom get two drinks.

Maybe that's all she can afford, she thought. With compassion in her heart, Sally stepped up to the register and discreetly told the cashier that she was paying for the two slushies this mother was getting. Sally left, grateful that she was in a place in her life to be able to pay it forward.

One week later, she stopped at the same store for another fountain drink. When she went to pay, the cashier said, "Hey, you're the lady who paid for that mom's stuff last week, aren't you?"

"Yes," Sally said.

The cashier excitedly asked, "You know who she was, don't you?"

"No," Sally replied.

Again, the cashier asked, "You know who that was don't you?"

Again, Sally said, "No."

The cashier's words quickly spilled out as she told this story: "The mom came up to pay, and I told her, 'An angel has already taken care of your purchase.' She usually doesn't come into this store as she never has much money. That day she came in because she just felt like she needed to do something special for her kids. It's so sad . . ."

"What happened?"

The cashier said, "She and her children left that afternoon not knowing it would be one of the last things she would ever do for her children. She was killed that very night in car accident."

When Sally heard this, God immediately brought to her mind the words of Matthew 25:40: "The King will reply, 'Truly I tell you, whatever you did for one of the least of these brothers and sisters of mine, you did for me.'" Hearing this message from the Lord, through His Word that she had treasured in her heart, gave Sally great peace. She knew she had served her Father well.

When God brought that Scripture to her memory, it may have been His way of saying thank you for the kindness she had shown this young mom. Perhaps it was to remind her to always be kind, for we never know what lies ahead. It was like a kiss of approval from her King when God used a Scripture to speak to Sally that she had lodged in her heart long before.

The other gal, Brenda, shared with me how she woke up one night overcome by a feeling of great fear. It was a very real fear, something she could not simply shake off as a bad dream. "It was like I was battling something," she said.

Brenda immediately began to pray. In her prayer, she began quoting chapters and verses in the Bible—just the places where the verses were found. She couldn't remember what the actual Scriptures said, so she pulled out her Bible to see what she was praying.

She first turned to Psalm 23:1: "The Lord is my shepherd, I lack nothing." The next verse was Isaiah 41:13: "For I am the Lord your God who takes hold of your right hand and says to you, 'Do not fear; I will help you.'" And the last one she was praying was 2 Timothy 1:7: "For the spirit God gave us does not make us timid, but gives us power, love, and self-discipline."

Talk about a great series of Scriptures to be praying when you're fighting something in the dark! Brenda did not even know what she was praying! God brought Bible references to her mind during a battle, a spiritual warfare battle. At some point, she had read these verses and just tucked them away. She did not recall ever meditating on them or specifically committing them to memory, but she had. God brought them to her memory when she needed them most and spoke to her through His Word. When the battle was warring against her in the middle of the night, He gave her the weapons she needed to fight through that fear.

Perhaps you have a story with a similar ending. God uses Scripture to speak to us. We recognize His voice in it, because it is His Word that we have hidden in our hearts. This is like a beautiful circle of love: God gave us the Word, we read the Word, He brings it to our minds in time of need, and we recognize His voice through the written Word.

Alive to Give Life

Have you ever heard God's Word called the "living Word?" It really is! Hebrews 4:12 says, **"For the word of God is alive and active. Sharper than any double-edged sword, it penetrates even to dividing soul and spirit, joints and marrow; it judges the thoughts and attitudes of the heart."** His Word is alive and active!

What does that even mean?

I love the way *The Message* Bible translates this verse. It says, "God means what he says. What he says goes. His powerful Word is sharp as a surgeon's scalpel, cutting through everything, whether doubt or defense, laying us open to listen and obey."

Wow! He means what He says, and what He says goes. Sounds just like an earthly father! Or maybe our earthly dads have been quoting Scripture all along, and we just never knew. I am sure my dad was not the only dad who ever reminded his children in a rather loud and grumpy voice, "I'm the dad, and what I say goes!"

The part about God's Word being like a surgeon's scalpel is powerful. God's Word will lay us open to listen. God uses His Word to get us ready us to hear His voice, to listen, so we will obey.

We spend a great deal of time reading the Word; we study it either on our own or maybe in group Bible studies or even in Sunday school or worship service. Sometimes, the words we read seem to leap off the page and scream, "Hello! Are you listening to me?" It's like a big neon flashing sign that says, "Look here!" with a huge pointing arrow. When this happens, it is God speaking to you at that exact moment. He is meeting with you in the here and now, right where you are.

When that happens to me, I read and then reread the verse. I usually highlight it and make a note in my margin about how God spoke to me about the situation it applied to so it will serve as a record of the time. I read everything around it so I understand the context of the verse. I may even pull out my parallel Bible so I can read other versions of the Scripture. They sometimes help me break it down for easier understanding. If we take time to get alone and quiet ourselves before Him, God can bless us with these neon moments.

The Word is alive in church too. Perhaps you have left a Sunday worship service almost angry because the preacher put all your business out on the platform that day. You know those messages I am talking about—the ones where it seems the minister is speaking directly to you as if he had been attached at your hip the past dreadful week, and now he is laying it all out and seemingly telling the world. In fact, he has no idea what you have been through this week and was in no way pointing any fingers at you, but the conviction of the message was hitting you square between the eyes. The Word was alive right then and there, speaking into your current circumstances.

There are those times in our Bible studies and devotions that we just seem to be going through the motions and answering the study questions and may not feel it applies to our current life situations. Fast-forward a few days, months, or perhaps years, and you find yourself ministering to someone in need. You may feel you have nothing to offer as you have never walked that person's road. But suddenly, that study you did fifteen years ago comes to your mind. The Scriptures you studied seem to come rolling off your tongue offering hope to this hurting soul. You catch yourself having one of those, "Where did that come from?" kind of moments. Has that ever happened to you?

This is an example of what it means for the Word to be the *living Word*. It was there, lodged in the recesses of your mind. But when it was needed, it was like hidden treasure bursting forth with new life. You took the Word into your heart, and at the right time and place, God used it to speak to someone through you. What a gift from God.

Do you make a weekly grocery list so you don't forget that all-important, recipe-changing ingredient? How much more important is it to have Scripture in our minds so God can recall it to us during a moment of crisis so it can be used to edify, uplift, and encourage a friend during a battle? Are you hiding treasures like golden nuggets of wisdom in the recesses of your mind? God's Word, His Scripture, is alive, and it's just waiting to speak not only to you but through you.

Gentle Rebuke

One last thought about hiding His Word in our hearts. Romans 12:2 tells us, "Do not conform to the pattern of this world but be transformed by the renewing of your mind. Then you will be able to test and approve what God's will is—his good, pleasing and perfect will." Do you ever test Him?

Do you ever wonder, Am I not partaking in this because the church or others say it's wrong, or is it because God says it's wrong? Maybe you have been raised in church your entire life, and you have never been one to buck the system or test the waters; you have just gone along with what you were taught.

Me? I have to test all waters. I must know in my heart and my mind that what I am doing or not doing is because God said so. I cannot make wise decisions by simply following someone else's lead, and neither should you. I guess I am much like the Berean Jews in Acts 17. When Paul spoke to them, they listened and received his message but took what he said and examined the Scriptures to see if what he said was true. They didn't just take him at his word. They sought confirmation through the Scriptures just as we should.

By hiding the Word in your heart, you can trust God to use those hidden words not only to encourage you but also to rebuke you if you are leaning left or right of what is good and pure in His eyes.

We were once in a place when money was beyond tight. There was little money for bills and even less for food. It just so happened that the lottery was at an all-time high when my faith was at an all-time low.

I said to God, "I don't need to win the whole thing, just enough to help us get out of this slump." I went out to purchase the ticket, and immediately God rebuked me by bringing Proverbs 28:19 to my mind. "Those who work their land will have abundant food, but those who chase fantasies will have their fill of poverty." He showed me I was chasing a fantasy, and I just needed to work a little harder.

Does this verse say anything about gambling? No, but it was what I needed at that moment; it was living and active. God uses the words we have hidden in our hearts to not only speak life to us but also to rebuke us when needed. Please understand this is my personal conviction, but it may not be yours, and that is okay.

Just to let you know how this lean time and rebuke played out: a few days later I went to my ministry post office box, which is usually only filled with sales fliers, and there was a card waiting. I opened it to find not only a word of encouragement but some cash. That was much-needed cash and right on time. A few days later, I went again to clean the sales ads out, and to my surprise, I found another envelope. This time, I pulled a piece of newspaper out and was utterly speechless when I found a check for $500 from a woman I have never met. God used her to bless me. I was reminded there is a season in life for *everything*! The current season in my life is to write this book and trust Him for all my needs.

Recognizing the Voice of the Shepherd

My shepherd friend Ray tells a story about a teenage shepherdess in the Middle East. A nearby flock was attacked and completely decimated by predators. The owner of the shepherdess's flock gave a ewe she had raised, along with some of his other sheep, to the shepherd whose flock had been decimated to help build it up.

Three years later, the shepherdess called out to her flock. She was surprised when she looked up and saw a fluffy, white ball of wool running to her from about a mile away, well out of the range of her current flock. As the distance closed between them, she realized the lamb running toward her was the little ewe she had not seen since she'd been given to another shepherd. Somehow, maybe the wind was blowing just right that day to carry her voice to the sheep. The little sheep heard the familiar voice that had called her home in her early life and went running to her. The lamb remembered her shepherdess; she remembered her voice, and she remembered her first home.

Will you, like the little lamb, recognize the voice of the Shepherd when He calls? If you cannot say yes with confidence, I urge you to draw closer to Him so you can change your sheepish "I'm not really sure" into a confident and bold "yes."

Scripture Focus

> Therefore put on the full armor of God, so that when the day of evil comes, you may be able to stand your ground, and after you have done everything, to stand. Stand firm then, with the belt of truth buckled around your waist, with the breastplate of righteousness in place, and with your feet fitted with the readiness that comes from the gospel of peace. In addition to all this, take up the shield of faith, with which you can extinguish all the flaming arrows of the evil one. Take the helmet of salvation and the

sword of the Spirit, which is the word of God. (Ephesians 6:13–17)

Let the word of Christ dwell in you richly in all wisdom; teaching and admonishing one another in psalms and hymns and spiritual songs, singing with grace in your hearts to the Lord. (Colossians 3:16 KJV)

I have hidden your word in my heart that I might not sin against you. (Psalm 119:11)

Challenge

I challenge you to commit to focus even more on hiding the Word of God in your heart by memorization, in order to have the tools needed to use His Word to speak to you. I further challenge you to become more like the Berean Jews and compare the messages you hear to the Scriptures. Make sure they are in agreement before you take it to heart.

Challenge Accepted

What will you do today to begin hiding the Word in your heart? One jump start idea: attach Scriptures to places like the bathroom mirror. This will be seen by everyone in your home—an automatic captive audience.

What specific Scripture will you commit to memory this week?

Will You Pray with Me?

Father God, I thank you for your living Word. I am thankful for a mind that can hold more than I can ever fathom, but I am ever grateful that you can pull those buried treasures out of me when they are most needed. Help me to be committed to hiding your Word in my heart, so you can use it to not only speak to me but also to speak your Word to others. In Jesus's name, amen.

FIVE

THE VOICES INSIDE OUR HEADS

I magine you are in the biggest department store in town, browsing the clearance section, looking for the deal you just can't turn down. You've only turned away from your child for a moment to find the right size, and when you look back, your five-year-old thrill seeker is gone. Poof! Vanished into thin air!

"Don't panic," you mutter under your breath. Trying to stay calm as you look through the aisles, you search first one aisle then two. Your heart quickens as you glance down the third aisle. On the fourth aisle, you begin to sweat a little, and your step quickens. Aisle five brings on full-on momma-bear mode, and you finally just scream out, "Johnny!"

Within seconds, Johnny pops up right behind you with his mischievous, toothless grin and responds, "Yah, Mom?" You embrace him, not sure whether to cry or scream at him.

Admit it, we all have had a moment like this in parenting. But guess what; little Johnny not only heard your voice when you called out, he also recognized it as *his* momma's voice and responded. He did so because he has been with you since birth; he spends time with you every single day. That is how a parent-child relationship works.

It is the very same way with our relationship with God. He is our Father, and we are His children. We can know His voice just as intimately as our children know ours.

Can you imagine how this story might have played out differently if Johnny hadn't recognized his mother's voice? After all the stranger-danger teachings little children receive, Johnny may very well have gone into hiding beneath the clothing racks, stayed as silent as a mouse, scared to death. Or perhaps he might have been that friendly child who never met a stranger and ended up being lured away by a sweet-sounding person who said she needed his help. That is a kind of chaos nightmares are made of.

Maybe you, too, follow voices that do not intend to lead you to good things or don't recognize the ones that do.

Momma's Grunts

When a new lamb is born on Ray Carman's farm, the new momma helps to bring breath into the life of her little one as she cleans the baby, licking away the amniotic sac and clearing the gunk away from its nostrils. While all this is going on, the ewe is making a distinctive sound while she is cleaning off the lamb—a low grunt unique to that mother. As she cleans her newborn lamb, she makes this noise over and over, and in so doing, establishes an intimate bond with her baby.

That grunt after birth is a very important part of the life of the new lamb. In a flock with many new lambs running through the fields or taking shelter in the shade, each mother will lift her head and call out to her baby with her unique sound. If it had not heard its mother's voice at birth, confusion would quickly set in as the lamb heard all the other mothers call for their offspring. Which voice should it listen to? The ewe and the lamb are bonded, and each lamb intimately knows its mother's call. Otherwise, it would be sheepish chaos.

There are voices for good or evil that can feed into our everyday lives, some of them causing chaos.

Viral Impact

To say that the viral video had an impact on my life would be a huge understatement. In just a matter of hours, I had thousands of messages from all over the world! I not only had messages on my actual Facebook post, but I received private messages as well as messages on the thousands of shares the video received. It was insanity in motion; I couldn't keep up with the number of them.

There were positive messages of affirmation about finding hope because God was watching out for the homeless man, messages saying thank you for speaking out about the great love of Jesus, and messages about people finding their way back to Him because of this simple act. Three people said they saw my video on the very day they planned to end their lives, and it brought them back to the love of God.

Here's a sampling of some of the messages that poured in:

> I have a daughter who is lost—drugs and stuff. She, too, is homeless. This morning going through my phone, you popped up. I listened. See, I think your testament was for me too, so that I know that even though her life is lost, God still takes care of her.

> I am going through a divorce and am lower than I've ever been in my life. That video touched me and showed me that no matter what, God is still with me and not to give up.

> Your post touched my heart deeply. I'm in the hospital having a PICC line put in to keep fluids and medicine in for our little baby due in August. I'm new in my faith and getting to God. A testimony like yours makes it so enjoyable and pushes me to [know] God is always working and ever-present in our lives.

> I have been having a lot of storms lately, and I needed to hear your testimony about how God is still alive.

> I have been going through the battle of my life, and I have failed in the faith the last couple of months. But today, praise God, I laid it down for the last time.

The outpouring of all these positive voices, feeding into the frenzy that has kept the video alive was just bananas.

"She Is Bananas!"

However, there was another side, a very dark side to this outpouring, a side I have not shared or commented on before. Among the comments were some hateful ones.

> She's a mental case!

> She needs to see a shrink for those voices in her head.

> Right, like there is a fairy godmother telling her to buy bananas. She *is* bananas.

This ugly list went on for nearly as long as the good comments did. It felt as if the people with negative comments were clamoring for my attention just the same as those sending love.

Once I'd read them, both sides of the comments ended up as voices in my head. On one side were voices lifting me up and encouraging me. On the other were voices trying to destroy not only my credibility but the credibility of God.

Flaming Arrows

During the days and weeks that followed, I took a very strong stance as to which voices I would listen to, or as I like to say, that I would allow to rent space in my cute little head.

To those who spewed hate, I simply fell silent. I did not remove ugly comments as everyone is entitled to his or her opinion. I simply ignored them.

You see, those who were being so negative were commenting *after* they had viewed the video. They had watched a three-and-half-minute video about the love of Christ. Whether they later added degrading comments or not, for that length of time, they listened while I shared the love of Jesus. Seeds were planted! I had heard and responded to God's voice, and then told others about it. My job was done. The way I see things, God used me to plant seeds of faith in many people through that simple act of kindness, though they did not even realize it.

Remember that full armor of God, the "sword of the Spirit," that is a part of the Christian's armor? Well, another vital piece of that armor is the shield of faith. Ephesians 6:16 says, "In addition to all this, take up the shield of faith, with which you can extinguish all the flaming arrows of the evil one." This became very personal to me as those hateful comments were flung my way. While I appeared silent to the masses, here is what was really happening.

As I read the ugly comments, I saw them as flaming arrows from the Evil One trying to destroy my act of obedience. Against each arrow, I took up my shield of faith in grand Wonder Woman style! It was as if I was raising my shield to the right and the left, going high and sinking to the ground for the low blows. With each deflection, I bounced back as I prayed, "Jesus, thank you for allowing me to plant a seed. Now I pray you will prepare the one that will be sent to cultivate the soil and then the one who will reap the harvest. I pray you will soften the heart of this individual so he or she may come to know the love of Christ. Amen."

Then, without shame, I'd giggle! I giggled because, whether they liked it or not, a seed had been planted. What they do with that seed is ultimately left up to them. I also giggled because my faith increased with each flaming arrow.

Have you ever heard that old saying, "If the Enemy ain't chasing you, he already has you?" Each ugly response was a voice of confirmation that I was on the right path.

What's in Your Head?

What kind of voices do you hear in your head? The last song you heard on the radio? Your favorite news anchor retelling the latest tragedy in your community? Perhaps the voice is a play-by-play of everything you saw today in social media? With our drive to be informed through Twitter, Instagram, Facebook, Tumblr, YouTube, Pinterest, and all the other social media sites, it is a wonder we can hear anything other than the voice of the world.

If this is what is filling your mind, you need an adult time-out!

Perhaps there is a self-imposed war being waged in your mind. Are you allowing the Enemy to keep throwing the fiery darts of past sins at you?

Perhaps you are allowing a seed of bitterness to take root in your heart and mind. You know, that bitterness you are harboring because someone else was chosen for the promotion over you even though you have been there longer.

Maybe you feel guilt over a failed relationship?

Are you thinking about a word spoken in anger to your loved one?

Maybe you are allowing feelings of worthlessness to creep in and cloud your self-image.

If these things are renting space in *your* cute little head, you, too, need an adult time-out, a time-out to serve some eviction notices to these thoughts of self-condemnation.

If so, I encourage you to take the time to get alone with your Father. I promise you, the world will not stop turning if you shut all the noise out for a while. Set aside time every day to read His Word, spend time with Him, and allow Him the opportunity to speak to you.

We can choose which voices we allow to fill our minds. Do you want to be filled with the rubbish of this world that does not profit you, or do you want to be filled with Scriptures and music that feed your soul and offer encouragement in your valleys?

Take the time to *actively* listen during your prayers. You will find when your heart is surrendered to Him, He will guide the very words of your prayers, and He *will* speak to you.

But you won't hear Him unless you serve an eviction notice to the other voices. How do we evict the toxic voices in our mind? This is easy for me to answer. Have you seen the movie, *War Room*? If not, put that on your immediate to-do list.

A good portion of this movie is about a husband and wife whose marriage is rocky at best. The husband is dealing with serious sin in his life. The wife desperately wants to save her marriage but is not sure what all the issues at hand are. So she goes to the Word of God. Using Scripture, she devises a battle plan of prayer to save her marriage. She hits her knees in prayer, and she cries out to God to "move the mountain." When she feels the power of God rising up within her, she starts walking through their home, screaming at the devil, and quoting the verses she has been praying. With each Scripture, her voice gets louder, her conviction stronger.

And then it happens. She goes to the back door, opens it, and *throws the devil out*! She tells the devil in no uncertain terms, "Get out and stay out!"

Sound extreme? Maybe. But it is exactly what I do when I need to evict any form of toxicity in my life. With the authority of Christ, I march through my house and serve notice to all the forces of evil that are trying to come against me. I declare that all in my house will serve the Lord. I say, "There is no room for the Evil One or any of his friends."

Then I pull out the knockout punch found in John 1:5: "The light shines in the darkness, and the darkness cannot overcome it." Jesus is the Light. Satan comes to destroy the light in us and render us dark. But the Word says darkness cannot overcome the Light!

After I call out specific things I need to remove from my mind and heart, I start saying the name *Jesus* over and over. At the name of Jesus, the introduction of Light, the devil must flee—he cannot overcome Jesus!

Opinion versus Wise Counsel

Always be attentive to the voices you allow to speak into your life, the ones you let inside your head, and the ones you invite to speak to your ears and heart. Not everyone has your best interests in mind. Like the wolf in sheep's clothing, there are some great pretenders out there, and they lie in wait for the opportunity to lead you astray and devour you.

Then there is the "good" advice that might not be God advice.

How do you handle touchy situations in your life? Most of us may invoke our right to phone a friend—best friend, that is.

The conversation starts out something like this: "Girl, let me tell you what so-and-so is trying to get me to do." Or, "Sister, you're not gonna believe what so-and-so said to me at church on Sunday."

This conversation is already doomed. Let me call a spade a spade. This is gossip central disguised as a prayer request.

I know how this goes. We have situations come up, and we feel hurt. We need help navigating murky waters, so we reach out for some advice.

Let's face it; typically, our best friends *are* our best friends, because we are like-minded. If you have been besties for long, you have already developed a track record of always having each other's backs. Best friends usually will "fight to the death" for one another, even if they are in the wrong. We love to share and commiserate with our bestie, because they allow us to. They take our sides, they stand up for us, and they go to bat for us. But in all honesty, our best friends may not be the best place to run when we need godly counsel. What? Yes, more often than not, our best friends will tell us what we *want* to hear not what we *need* to hear.

When life comes at us with what I like to call a plot twist, the first thing we need to do is pray and read the Bible for direction. Sometimes, even if we do read the Bible and pray, we may still feel confused or unsure of what the right action or reaction should be.

It is then that we need to seek the counsel of wise, godly folks around us. This may be your pastor, your pastor's wife, or perhaps a mentor. Proceed with caution. Pray and ask God to lead you to whomever He would have you speak.

Proverbs 12:5–6 warns us: "The plans of the righteous are just, but the advice of the wicked is deceitful. The words of the wicked lie in wait for blood, but the speech of the upright rescues them." This verse immediately takes me to another one found in 1 Peter 5:8, "Be alert and of sober mind. Your enemy, the devil, prowls around like a roaring lion looking for someone to devour."

God uses those with wisdom greater than ours as His voice to speak to us. If you think this plot twist in your life needs some intervention, make sure you seek counsel from an individual of good moral character who demonstrates sound values. Then take the counsel given and compare it to Scripture just like the Berean Jews did. Does Scripture support the advice given for the situation?

This is one of the ways God speaks to you. He uses the counsel of others to give you direction. If it lines up with the Bible, that is His direct confirmation to you.

Do you have a plan of action for times like this? Do you have a pastor or mentor you can reach out to with confidence that he or she will guide you on a path that will be pleasing to God? If you don't, I encourage you to be praying about this. The worst time to devise a healthy plan is in the middle of a crisis.

A dear friend in ministry shared the following story with me about a time she received godly counsel from a friend who spoke the Lord's truth into her life and situation.

"In 1998, in my first year of ministry, I went to an associate pastors' retreat in Kansas City. I had left elementary education to take a youth ministry position—quite a switch from teaching kindergarten students to working with teenagers. I was already in my late twenties and felt like the natural path was for me to transition into children's ministry within a few years. After all, I wasn't getting any younger. How long could I expect to do all-nighters and keep up with teenagers? I have never been athletic and always considered myself to be a very non-traditional youth pastor—not young, not hip, not cool by any stretch of the imagination.

"One of the leaders at the retreat was a youth pastor in his fifteenth year of ministry. He sat down with me one day and asked about my plans for the future. When I told him I anticipated only doing youth ministry for a few years, he challenged me. He said most youth pastors stay in the same location an average of eighteen *months*, which provides no stability for students. He quoted statistics saying that the best and most effective years of ministry don't happen until a youth pastor reaches five to eight *years* in the same location. He encouraged me to stay with youth ministry for the long haul provided I didn't feel a very clear move away from this area by the Holy Spirit.

"I took his words to heart, and time has proven that what he said was true. I stayed in the same ministry position for seventeen years and found that it just got better and better. I loved youth ministry from day one, and my love for students continued to grow.

"When I sensed God was taking me in a different direction, I was sad. I submitted my resignation, not knowing what I was to do next. I couldn't imagine doing anything but youth ministry, but finding myself in my mid-forties, I knew most churches would not be interested in hiring someone my age for this type of position.

"I tried to think outside the box; I looked at para-church ministries and different types of pastoral positions. Nothing seemed right. Then, in another God-ordained conversation, I mentioned to a trusted friend in ministry that I would be a great person to serve in a right-hand position alongside a youth pastor. After all, I understood youth ministry, had knowledge and experience, and loved all aspects of it. This conversation sparked an idea inside in my colleague. His assistant had just made a move, and he thought that perhaps, with a little creativity, he could create a new position that would fit me very well.

"Three months later, I walked into the national office of a large religious organization with a partial job description and the title of North American Youth Ministries Project Coordinator. In the three years since, I have served in this role, helping to create life-changing events and learning opportunities for students and their leaders. I work closely with student interns and still take a mentoring role with students in the community. I am able to use my writing and teaching skills in multiple ways and provide support for many other areas of youth ministry. I am thankful that God orchestrates my life and always guides me by His perfect plan!"

God guided my friend through the words of another. That, too, is a way we hear His voice.

Still Strength in Numbers

Remember in chapter 3 when I talked about there being strength in numbers and how we need to gather together with like-minded individuals to weather the storms of life? As Proverbs 24:6 reminds us, "Surely you need guidance to wage war, and victory is won through many advisors."

When we are facing a particularly difficult situation or perhaps a life-changing decision, it may be wise to seek the counsel from a group of confidants, not just one. Don't automatically assume an attitude of majority rules when doing this. Yet often, when we seek the counsel of several, while they will not all give us the same advice, we'll find a common thread woven among the answers.

Again, proceed with caution and go back to the Word. A great place to start comparing the advice to Scripture is found in Philippians 4:8. Ask yourself if the advice you received is honest. Is it just? Is it pure? Everything always goes back to God's Word; it is the standard by which all our decisions, actions, and reactions will be judged. Psalm 119:105 says, "Your word is a lamp for my feet, a light on my path." With God's Word illuminating our every step, what better counsel could we ask for? If the advice you received aligns with Scripture and the sources are trustworthy, you will likely have heard your answer.

You may wonder, Am I weak if I go ask someone what I am supposed to do? I have served Christ for years, why do I need to ask someone else? Be encouraged; seeking counsel is a sign of maturity and humility. It is an acknowledgment that we are works in progress and will continue to grow in Christ until the day He calls us home.

It is also a sign of respect for our elders and the wisdom they desire to impart to us. I love Psalm 71:18 that says, "Even when I am old and gray, do not forsake me, my God, till I declare your power to the next generation, your mighty acts to all who are to come." There is so much wisdom to be absorbed from the generations before us. Take advantage of it, be encouraged by it, and when *you* are old and gray, pay it forward!

His Voice, the Only Voice

Remember the new momma sheep and her baby lamb? She took the time to make sure her little one intimately knew her voice, her grunts, so there would be no confusion in the field when the other new mothers called to their own offspring. God longs to do that same thing for each of us. When we are born again, He comes to us and wipes our sin and shame away so we can have new life in Him. He speaks softly and tenderly to us with His own unique call for each of us. You see, He knows we will hear many voices in our lifetimes, each one striving for the attention of His very own offspring, so He takes His time to form an intimate bond that will not be easily shaken by those who seek to destroy it.

If you will guard your heart against the voices that seek to distract you and get grounded in the Word of God, if you will learn to recognize His voice as easily as the little lamb recognized his momma's, I promise you God will fulfill the word found in 2 Thessalonians 3:3: "But the Lord is faithful, and he will strengthen you and protect you from the evil one." He will keep you to the end of the battles on this earth.

When you know His voice this well, you, too, will be like the little lamb. No matter how far away you may be, no matter how many other voices surround you, when He calls you, you *will* hear Him. The Enemy does not have a knockout punch in his arsenal when the voice of God is the only one you listen to.

Scripture Focus

> In addition to all this, take up the shield of faith, with which you can extinguish all the flaming arrows of the evil one. (Ephesians 6:16)

> Be alert and of sober mind. Your enemy the devil prowls around like a roaring lion looking for someone to devour. (1 Peter 5:8)

> Your word is a lamp for my feet, a light on my path. (Psalm 119:105)

Challenge

I challenge you to do a self-examination of the voices you allow to speak into your life. If necessary, take an adult time-out and serve some eviction notices. Then I encourage you to get alone with your Father and wait on Him to speak to your heart.

Challenge Accepted

Who are the voices who speak into your life? Looking at your list, consider whether that person is godly counsel or one who brings chaos.

To which voices do you need to serve eviction notices?

Go to the Scriptures, create your own battle plan, and begin to daily pray over them.

Thinking back to Proverbs 12:5–6, pray that God will protect your heart and mind from the advice of the wicked.

Will You Pray with Me?

Father God, I thank you for loving me so much that you want to spend time alone with me. Help me guard my heart and my mind against the voices that seek to distract me from your presence. Help me make the right choices when choosing the voices I will allow to influence my life. Help me be committed to spending quiet time with you and your Word every single day so I might draw close enough to always recognize your voice apart from all others. In Jesus's name, amen.

SIX

FALSE TEACHERS AND PROPHETS

Have you ever been in a situation where the leadership has whitewashed what was going on?

Whitewash, according to the *Merriam-Webster Dictionary*, means "quick, brief, hasty, superficial, careless, sketchy and inattentive." So, to whitewash means "to exonerate by means of a careless and inattentive investigation."

Or in Tammy-speak, a false teacher is one who chooses to act like nothing ever happened when situations arise rather than deal with it.

A friend of mine was once a part of her local church board and tells about a time when the teenage son of the music director was found to be involved in a rather awkward situation at the church. Many of the church members knew of the situation and that it was not the first time he was caught in the act. The parents' response to the situation was merely, "Boys will be boys."

The pastor, rather than deal with it head-on and offer the support of biblical counseling, simply ignored the situation and did not respond at all. On the occasions this happened, he acted as if it had never happened.

A false teacher may react with silence or perhaps cast the blame on someone else, diverting the negative attention away from themselves. They choose to whitewash over what happened. We don't need someone to whitewash the truth; we need someone who will speak the truth to us in love.

Wolves in Sheep's Clothing

Jesus warns us to be aware of the wolves who come in sheep's clothing. Mathew 7:15 says, "Watch out for false prophets. They come to you in sheep's clothing, but inwardly they are ferocious wolves."

Sheep will not follow a predator, but they will follow other sheep. Unfortunately, some wolves are dressed like sheep, sheep trained to lead other sheep astray. You may never see them coming if you're not standing guard.

Shepherd Ray tells how he was standing in a slaughter facility and observing the sheep. He says, "Before then, I had never really considered sheep. My attention was awakened, though, by one sheep who really stood out that day. They called him the Judas sheep. In any flock, that name was given to the sheep trained to lead the other sheep straight into the slaughter pens. Sheep naturally follow other sheep; therefore, this instinct is used against them to get them the through the slaughter process quickly and precisely."

Kiss of Betrayal

If you're not familiar with where the name *Judas* comes from, here is a brief explanation. Judas, one of the twelve disciples of Christ, is best known for his betrayal of Jesus. Judas had accepted a payment of thirty pieces of silver in exchange for handing Jesus over to the Sanhedrin, the religious authorities of the day, who were threatened by Jesus and wanted to see Him dead. Judas kissed Jesus to identify Him to the authorities.

A verse that stands out in the story of Judas is found in Matthew 26:56: "But this has all taken place that the writings of the prophets might be fulfilled."

This Scripture says to me that *Judas had to betray Jesus for the Scriptures to be fulfilled.*

If a Judas had to exist in the life of Jesus, what makes us think we will go through this life without facing a Judas of our own? We won't. We will all have a Judas at some point in our lives. We will all have one or more who will kiss us in greeting while trying to lead us astray on our journey for Christ, who will seek to harm us or use us for his own purposes. We must be ever watchful for the one who wishes to offer us a kiss of betrayal. How can we guard against such an encounter?

Profile of a False Teacher

What does recognizing wolves in sheep's clothing have to do with hearing the voice of God? Everything! We must learn to recognize the voice of God so we can be ever vigilant against the ones who, in disguise, try to imitate it.

What does a false teacher or prophet look like?

The most common characteristic of a false teacher is that they like to tickle our ears with what we want to hear versus what we need to hear. We read in Galatians 1:10: "Am I now trying to win the approval of human beings, or of God? Or am I trying to please people? If I were still trying to please people, I would not be a servant of Christ."

This reminds me of those who would rather keep the congregation happy and satisfied than to preach the hard truths of the gospel. It is much easier for me to reach in my wallet and willingly give when I am being told a grand story of love, grace, and mercy. Giving may be more difficult when I am being told the hard truths found in God's Word, such as God is a jealous God (Exodus 20:5) and He wants to be first and foremost in your life or not at all. John 3:16, perhaps the most beloved verse in the Bible, tells us, "God so loved the world that he gave his one and only Son, that whoever believes in him shall not perish but have eternal life."

Perish, according to the *Merriam-Webster Dictionary*, means to "suffer death, typically in a violent, sudden or untimely way or to suffer complete ruin or destruction." We don't want to hear about anyone perishing! Sign me up; I believe in Him. While this is one truth that will bring peace to us, we must also read Revelation 3:16: "So, because you are lukewarm—neither hot nor cold—I am about to spit you out of my mouth." A false teacher who wants to tickle our ears and make us feel all warm and fuzzy will perhaps leave that little tidbit of gospel out.

God sent His one and only Son just for you. But He does have expectations of us as His followers. We must guard against those who would sway us to our harm by luring us with stories that tell us only what we want to hear.

Puppy Dogs, Rainbows, and Lollipops

A life lived for Christ is not all puppy dogs, rainbows, and lollipops. There will be times when God will prune us to grow us. As seen in John 15:2, "He cuts off every branch in me that bears no fruit, while every branch that does bear fruit he prunes so that it will be even more fruitful." We need to have our trust in teachers of the gospel who will bring forth not only messages of hope but also messages that will be useful for pruning. Because without pruning, we will not grow!

We must also be wary of the one who brings a message that is full of "I believe" or "I don't believe" statements. Ezekiel 13:3 reads, "This is what the Sovereign Lord says: woe to the foolish prophets who follow their own spirit and have seen nothing!" While there are some things in life that are not clear in the Scriptures, if you know the voice of God, you will find your answer.

Remember when I told you about my lottery experience? Although Scripture does not specifically say do not play the lottery, in that moment and in that situation, God used His Word to speak to me; that's how I knew it was true. When teachers begin to teach what they think or what they believe to be the truth versus teaching us directly from the Scriptures, they are not being used of God and are foolish.

A little further down in Ezekiel 13:6–7 we read, "Their visions are false and their divinations a lie. Even though the Lord has not sent them, they say, 'the Lord declares,' and expect him to fulfill their words. Have you not seen false visions and uttered lying divinations when you say, 'The Lord declares,' though I have not spoken?"

A false teacher will be exposed over time as the prophecies they speak return void. One who has received the gift of prophecy will often have a reputation that precedes him. Remember the service I attended where I was told before even entering the church that if this man prophesies over you, you can take it to the bank? His reputation, his track record, for lack of better words, was proven over time. People had witnessed countless prophecies from him that have been fulfilled. They had no doubt that this was one whom God had chosen.

If you listen to someone claiming to speak for God, but what he says does not come to pass or align with God's Word, he is a false teacher.

Remember Tom Sawyer and how he got his fence whitewashed? He's not the only one that thinks whitewashing is a good idea; false teachers do too. Ezekiel 13:10–12 says:

> Because they lead my people astray saying "Peace," when there is no peace, and because, when a flimsy wall is built, they cover it with whitewash, therefore, tell those that cover it with whitewash that

it is going to fall. Rain will come in tor-
rents and I will send hailstones hurtling
down, and violent winds will burst forth.
When the wall collapses, will people not
ask you, "Where is the whitewash you
covered it with?"

An alternate definition of *whitewash* is "to exonerate
by means of a perfunctory investigation or through a *bi-
ased presentation* of data."

Where's the Fruit?

In 2 Peter 2, we find some very strong language about false
teachers and the destruction they bring. In this chapter,
I am focusing more on the character and conduct of the
false teacher and not the teachings themselves. Once you
recognize a false teacher, you know his or her teaching is
not right or is a mix of right and wrong. When we look
at the character and conduct of a teacher, we should consider them in the light of Matthew 7:16–20.

By their fruit you will recognize them.
Do people pick grapes from thorn bushes
or figs from thistles? Likewise, every good
tree bears good fruit, but a bad tree bears
bad fruit. A good tree cannot bear bad
fruit, and a bad tree cannot bear good
fruit. Every tree that does not bear good
fruit is cut down and thrown into the

fire. Thus, by their fruit you will recognize them.

With that in mind, let's take a closer look at 2 Peter 2:1–2.

> But there were also false prophets among the people, just as there will be false teachers among you. They will secretly introduce destructive heresies, even denying the sovereign Lord who bought them—bringing swift destruction on themselves. Many will follow their depraved conduct and will bring the way of truth into disrepute.

In verse 1, we find that "they will secretly introduce destructive heresies, even denying the sovereign Lord." Those words *secretly introduce* should quicken us to pay close attention. False teachers are not going to come to us wearing a billboard sign that says, "Here I am. I come to kill, rob, and destroy you!" They come dressed just like you and me and can be so very subtle as they "secretly introduce" false teachings to lead us astray.

As we read on in 2 Peter 2, we find false teachers are greedy, bold, arrogant, and even abusive while promising us freedom. A false teacher is not a savory character. We need spiritual eyes to guard against falling prey to such individuals or religious movements.

Spiritual Eyes

The first 3-D movie I saw was about race cars, and there were lots of fast and sudden movements. Oh boy, I was so excited as I sat down in my luxury recliner and kicked back with my popcorn, soda, and favorite movie snacks: Twizzlers and Milk Duds. With great expectation, I put those sexy 3-D glasses on and watched the screen. It felt as if I were driving one of those race cars, shifting gears, and flying around the turns at breakneck speeds, and I was almost giddy with excitement. But then it happened.

I was paying close attention to my every turn and watching cars go around me and cars nudging me from behind. They were going so fast—and in circles! The signs on the side of the track began to blur, one merging into the next. I felt as if I, too, was going so very fast—and in circles. My head started spinning, my stomach churning. *Uh-oh! I think I am going to be sick!* All because a pair of glasses brought the screen to life? Yes!

Do you know God wants to gift you a special set of eyes—spiritual eyes? These eyes won't make you unwell, but they will bring things to life. You've heard the saying about looking at life through rose-colored glasses. Imagine, if you will, that instead of being rose-colored lenses, the lenses are covered in the Word. With them, everything you look at is filtered by the Word of God. These are your spiritual eyes.

How do you get spiritual eyes?

When you become intimate with God's Word, you will come to know His voice as well as you know your own. When you allow your recognition of His voice and the knowledge of His Word to be the filter through which all teachings flow, you will be able to rest assured you are not falling prey to a false teacher. Knowing the Word of God and testing everything against it will guard against the wolf in sheep's clothing.

No matter what circumstance or what people we come up against—or alongside—in life, we must filter all through the Word. If a teaching or leading contradicts the Word or does not line up in any way, it is to be tossed out like yesterday's rubbish. Do not let false teachers rent space in your head or their words and actions take up residency in your heart. These teachers will lead you down a path of ultimate destruction as seen in 2 Peter 2.

Hide the Word and use it to your advantage. Learn to recognize and heed that gentle nudge when something seems off. Use it to recognize the actions of the Judas sheep who seek to lead you and your fellow believers astray by pretending to be one of you. Become so confident in knowing God's voice that you instantly recognize when the seductive tactics of the enemy comes and tries to lead you astray by masquerading as one of the flock. Be alert and listen, my friends, for God has given us a warning to this tactic of the enemy. If we are not careful, we may find ourselves following a Judas to the slaughtering grounds of sin and destruction.

Scripture Focus

> Watch out for false prophets. They come to you in sheep's clothing, but inwardly they are ferocious wolves. (Matthew 7:15)

He cuts off every branch in me that bears
no fruit, while every branch that does
bear fruit he prunes so that it will be even
more fruitful. (John 15:2)

For they mouth empty, boastful
words and, by appealing to the lustful desires of the flesh, they entice people who
are just escaping from those who live in
error. (2 Peter 2:18)

Challenge

Today, I challenge you to be ever watchful, ever praying
about those who you allow to speak in to your life, to
always weigh what they say against the Word. I challenge
you to further study the messages brought before you, to
dig a little deeper. Look into a Bible study on this par-
ticular subject or perhaps seek the counsel of the saints
around you.

Challenge Accepted

What was the message brought before you in your church
service this week? What was the Scripture focus of that
message? Did the message the minister brought align
with the Scriptures as you read and study them? If you
haven't looked them up and read them in context, will
you?

When you think about those whom you allow to
speak into your life, pray and ask God to reveal any toxic

relationships you may be involved in, and ask Him to help you set healthy boundaries in these relationships.

Will You Pray with Me?

Father God, thank you for your living Word, alive and active in my heart and life. I pray, Lord, as I hide your words in my heart, that you would use them to help me know if I am allowing any false teachings to cloud my journey with you. I pray I would be able to see any wickedness that comes against me and recognize the one who may come at me with an air of seduction, trying to lure me down a path of destruction. I put my trust and faith in you and you alone. In Jesus's name, amen.

SEVEN

WHEN GOD IS SILENT

In the past, I have served as an executive assistant to several individuals. When I interviewed for the positions, I was always very up front with my potential employer. I would say something like, "If you want someone you can hand a task to and know the task is as good as done, I am your match. But if you are someone who likes to micromanage a task, please let me know so we can end this interview now. I am not someone who can be micromanaged." I know that about myself! I am aware of how God wired me, and I understand both the conditions that I thrive in and the conditions that will destroy me and make me unproductive as an employee.

Once hired and the executive and I begin working well together, a point of trust is reached where tasks are handed off to me with the confidence they will be completed. I show my respect to my boss with one little word, four simple letters sent in an email. Done. D-O-N-E. Those four letters tell my boss I have completed the task he gave me. They keep him from wondering later if I finished the task or if something occurred that made me forget about the assignment. The one-word email is a simple confirmation that puts the boss's mind at ease. If a project is underway but not yet completed, I'd also send an update so he would know progress is being made and I haven't forgotten any details.

Don't you wish God had email so we'd have confirmation that He is at work on our requests? We might email Him, "I don't mean to take up your time, God, but I was just wondering if you are working on that thing I asked you about last week."

Ding! You have a new email: "Done."

Or perhaps the occasional return email would read, "In process." What a thought! A progress report from God to set our minds at ease. Wouldn't that be a dream come true?

But we all know that's not how it works in real life. We may go through periods—long periods—where we feel we are not hearing anything from our Father. We may begin to wonder if our connection to God is clogged.

You might wonder, Have I sinned against you? Is that why you are hiding your face from me? Is that why I can't hear your voice? We may begin to feel our prayers are bouncing off the proverbial glass ceiling above us.

Let's take a deeper look at those times of deafening silence.

Deafening Silence

When the progress report fails to come, my first step is to examine myself for the possible reasons for this seemingly silent time. I take a self-inventory and ask if I have done something that is hindering my communication with my Father? Is there a clog in the plumbing? I go into a reflective time of prayer and ask God to examine me and show me anything that may be standing in the way. When He does, if He does, I repent, and I wait.

If I feel no conviction of sin, I consider perhaps God is using silence to draw me even closer to Him.

At times, I will fast. This is something I am not seeing preached a lot about in the church today. According to Mark 9:29 (KJV), "And He said unto them, this kind can come forth by nothing, but by prayer and fasting."

There are some occasions where we need to not only pray but fast as well. Some things come only by prayer and fasting. The *Merriam-Webster Dictionary* definition of *fasting* is "to abstain from food." Fasting is not abstaining from social media; it is not just giving up Starbucks or Baskin-Robbins for a time. Fasting is depriving your body of food. When you should be eating lunch with your coworkers, you instead retreat to a private spot or to your car and spend that time in prayer. You are deliberately sacrificing your mealtime to draw closer to your Father in heaven. This may be one day; it may be three days. When you enter a time of prayer and fasting, ask God for direction, and He will give it to you.

During the times where God seems quiet, I challenge you to look around for where He is at work. Sometimes He is not silent, He is just using other forms of communication we may fail at first to recognize.

He might send a sunrise that wakes you and fills you with peace for your day. Perhaps He will send a sunset to blanket you in beautiful shades of pinks and purples as you stroll along the beach with your loved one. He may speak through a beautiful snowfall that covers the ground and shines like diamonds when the sun hits it, reminding us that though our sins may be as scarlet, they shall be white as snow.

Some of the hardest times to endure as a Christian are when you have prayed, and you know nothing is standing in the way of your communication with God, but still He seems silent. These times are made more difficult as we live in a right-now kind of world. Everything is instant from rice and microwave popcorn to the new and popular Instapot. We all want everything *now*. God is not microwave safe, and He does not always provide instant satisfaction to us. But we can count on Him being always right on time. Maybe not *your* time or *my* time but definitely *on* time.

While His voice may be silent to our ears, He must never become silent to our hearts. We will hear His voice in our hearts if we cling to and *hold unswervingly* to His Word. Start with the promise we find in Hebrews 13:5: "Never will I leave you; never will I forsake you." Hold on! The answer is coming.

Why must we endure these times of silence? Perhaps the answer is in the silence. Maybe His answer to your prayer is a simple no. Maybe the answer is "not yet." Whatever the reason, we must maintain our faith in Him and trust that His way is the best way. If He says no, it is for the best.

Have you ever seen that little cartoon picture of Jesus and a little girl, and Jesus is asking her to give Him the little stuffed bear she is holding?

She says to Jesus, "But I love it!" as she clutches the bear even tighter.

Jesus says to her, "Just trust me."

He is asking her to give Him something that means so very much to her—and to trust Him. What she cannot see is that behind His back He is holding a much bigger, much better bear for her. But she can't hold both. She must have enough trust and faith in Jesus to let go of what *she* wants and trust that what He has for her is far superior to what she is currently holding.

Sometimes, we don't hear His voice because we don't want to hear what He has to say. Or we hear Him but don't acknowledge it. Perhaps the Lord is asking you to do something, and you don't understand why. Just because we can't visualize the outcome does not mean we should not step out in faith and be obedient to the direction He is giving us.

If there is silence, it may be that He is waiting for us to respond to what He has already said.

One thing is sure, the silent times can be faith-building times if we allow them to be. God's Word never changes. His promises never change. If He has given you a promise about something, write it down and hold on to it! God is not a liar—He is not even capable of telling a lie.

Being a shepherd is not just a pastime or something you can do on the side, according to our shepherd friend, Ray. Being a good shepherd requires work every day. Sheep are fragile and easily lost if you do not keep a close eye on them. Left to themselves, they quickly become wild in nature, sick from parasites, and they will be easy prey for the predators.

Each day, Ray goes out to make sure there is plenty for the sheep to eat, especially during the winter months when they rely on delivered hay. He makes sure they have adequate and clean water to quench their thirst. At times, this means making sure a nearby pond is accessible and not frozen over, while at other times it means hauling water in pails out to a trough from which they may drink. He must watch the sheep's health, constantly checking for parasites, illnesses, and potential foot problems.

Again, the similarities between us and the sheep do not disappoint; instead, they instruct. We, too, require daily attention from our Father. We ask Him to watch over and keep us safe as we travel; we ask Him to guard us through the night as we sleep. We ask our Good Shepherd to place a hedge of protection around our children so they are safe when we are apart from them. We ask so many things of Him that require His attention every single day. He not only tends to our requests but to the needs He knows we have but of which we may not be aware. He does all these things daily! But, sometimes, He does them in silence. And that can be unnerving to us as believers.

Jesus is our Shepherd, and He tends to His flock—us—every day whether we see Him, hear Him, or not. Jesus did not just come to live, die, arise, and return to await our homecoming. No, He said He would be working daily to prepare the way before us. His work is never ending as He leads us to green pastures, beside still waters, and even through the dark valleys of shadows. He is at work every single day, tending to the needs of His flock. Even when He is silent, He is working!

I have a portion of Scripture highlighted in my Bible. Next to that highlighted verse, I have written the words "Dad's salvation." Tucked in my Bible next to that highlight is a receipt from Burger King for a ham, egg, and cheese croissant, hash browns, and a diet soda. I noted that reference right on the receipt in blue ink because of God's promise to me.

One morning after I dropped off my daughter at school, I stopped by Burger King, grabbed breakfast, and went to the local park to do my devotions.

As I was praying for my dad's salvation, God took me to that Scripture reference and laid out exactly how my dad will be saved. He gave me that promise in April 1997. Has it happened yet? Nope. Do I still believe it will? Without a doubt! God gave me a promise to hold on to, and I am holding fast to it. After speaking to me in the park, God has been silent on this subject for twenty-one years! But I have a promise to hold on to.

Learning to Tarry

Have you heard that old-fashioned word *tarry*? The *Merriam-Webster Dictionary* defines *tarry* as "to linger with great expectation." Lingering with *great* expectation is quite possibly one of the hardest things to do as a follower of Christ! We pray and expect God to answer us immediately, but His response is silence. Those are the times when He is beckoning us to simply quiet ourselves before Him and "linger with great expectation."

Great *expectation*?

Tucked away and hidden in the back of a bottom store shelf, you find Tickle Me Elmo—the *only* toy your child asked for at Christmas. You are excited and relieved all at the same time. You were one of the lucky ones to find this popular item. You take it home and hide it in the secret place, waiting for Christmas morning. You spend the next weeks waiting with *great expectation* to see the reaction of your child.

We need to long for God's presence and wait for His answers with great expectation until the very day He returns to take us home.

A great example of learning to linger can be found in the book of Habakkuk. Habakkuk was a prophet in the Old Testament who experienced the prosperity and promise of spiritual renewal given to Judah, but he also witnessed its decline. Habakkuk had a conversation with God, but God did not answer all the questions the prophet had. He did assure him He was in complete control and would remain in control until the very end. In Habakkuk 3, we read the prayer of the prophet as he proclaims, "The Sovereign Lord is my strength!" He says this no matter what.

How often do we complain before the Lord saying, "Lord, are you listening to me? I am so confused, and I need help."

Habakkuk complained to God about why God was tolerating violence and wrongdoing. In Habakkuk 1:13 he says, "Your eyes are too pure to look on evil; you cannot tolerate wrongdoing. Why then do you tolerate the treacherous? Why are you silent while the wicked swallow up those more righteous than themselves?"

Don't we wonder ourselves why God is silent?

God's reply in this conversation is the best. Habakkuk 2:2–3 reads, "Then the Lord replied: 'Write down the revelation and make it plain on tablets so that a herald may run with it. For the revelation awaits an appointed time; it speaks of the end and will not prove false. Though it linger, wait for it; it will certainly come and will not delay.'"

Allow me to break this down even further.

"The revelation awaits an appointed time" means the answer is coming, but it is not time to reveal it yet. "It speaks of the end and will not prove false" means the answer will tell you exactly how this is going to go down, and it *will* happen just like I will tell you. "Though it linger, wait for it; it will certainly come and will not delay."

God is telling us that if we wait, we will get the answer to our questions. But we *must* wait as it is not yet time to bring it about. But once He gives us this answer, it will come quickly; it will not delay.

God is not silent during times when we do not receive an answer.

If you have ever watched my videos on Facebook, you know I have a saying—maybe some would call it a quirk. If I am trying to think of something and having trouble remembering it, or if I go to my Bible to look something up quickly while live on camera, I will raise my hand and press my thumb together with my index finger, look at the camera, and say, "Please hold."

Imagine at these seemingly silent times that God is looking at you and saying, "Please hold." He is not ignoring us; He is just not ready to deliver the answer quite yet. His timing is always perfect!

Faith in Action

Have you ever read chapter 11 of the book of Hebrews? I don't mean just read *through* it, I mean really read it, studied it, and absorbed it. Do you live it? If you are not familiar with it, I would encourage you to really dig into that book and chapter in full.

Verse 7 says, "By faith Noah, when warned about things not yet seen, in holy fear built an ark to save his family. By his faith he condemned the world and became heir of the righteousness that is in keeping with faith."

Many have heard the story of Noah; some have not. If you were brought up in church or ever helped at a Vacation Bible School you have likely sung about Noah building his ark. But have you ever taken the time to dig a little deeper into the story of Noah and the ark?

There is one truth about that ark that blows my mind.

I had long thought the words "things not yet seen" referred to the coming flood that was going to destroy the earth.

If God said to you today, "I am going to flood the earth again, and you need to get ready," you'd make things waterproof, store some food, buy a houseboat, and get to higher ground. You might not have all the knowledge needed, but you would understand the consequences if you failed to be prepared.

Many Bible scholars believe that when God spoke to Noah and told him He was going to bring floodwaters to all the earth, it had never even rained before. Are they right? I can't answer that with absolute certainty, so I have tucked this into my questions-for-when-I-reach-heaven file.

He couldn't google the meaning of *flood*. He simply took God at His word that He was going to destroy everything on earth. Later, Noah trusted God when He said He would establish a covenant with him, a promise that this was a one-time event. He would never again destroy the earth by flood.

Why do we find taking God at His word so hard? Not only did God make this promise to Noah, but He sends us a reminder of this promise every time a rainbow appears in the sky according to Genesis 9:13.

God gave some very detailed building directions for the ark to Noah. Do you think Noah even understood what an ark was? I doubt it. I imagine it would be about as likely for him to have known as it would have been for me to understand the words *cellular device* back in 1972.

God gave him the exact dimensions of the ark, what wood to use, instructions to divide it into three levels, and how many of each animal with which to fill the ark. He told him who would be permitted in the ark. In Genesis 6:22, we find that "Noah did everything just as God commanded him." He didn't take shortcuts or use a different wood because it was cheaper. He didn't leave certain creatures behind because they would make a huge mess. No, God gave instructions, and Noah followed them to the letter.

This screams to me, personally, to stop trying to find the shortcut to the destiny God has for me! I am going to have to work and work hard on this road, but it will be worth it all.

I imagine this time in Noah's life was full of bullying from the townspeople as they watched what was taking place. They didn't have directions from God, and they didn't know about the impending floodwaters. I don't read any account where God came back to Noah and encouraged him along the way. I don't find God telling him to ignore the hecklers. I don't read where He said, "Great job, Noah! Keep it up. Only forty-three days until the rain comes. Keep pressing forward." No encouragement, no reminders, no additional words.

Yet Noah persisted in silence in the task God called him to accomplish.

Just like my hope and trust in God for my dad's salvation, Noah put all his hope and trust in the Lord.

The silent times cannot distract us from the call. We must keep to the task at hand and trust God's way is perfect.

In Genesis 7, we read that the rain came, and it rained for forty days. The earth was covered in flood water for 150 days, and the flood waters were so deep they covered even the tops of the mountains. Now think about this: how hard did it have to rain during those forty days to cover all the earth including the mountain tops? I imagine they were ferocious, torrential downpours not an on-again-off-again rain. I visualize the ugliest storm this earth has ever endured. I see high winds and the ark being tossed about on the rolling waves, perhaps being thrust into treetops and mountainsides. Is this how it happened? We have no way of really knowing. We can only imagine. But I do know that was a whole lot of rain in a short amount of time.

I imagine this storm and the water, the tossing of the boat. I see hay flying up in the air and Noah and his family strapped in like flight attendants during takeoff. It's a crazy scene playing out in my mind. Perhaps during the worst of the storm, the momma bear in Noah's wife rears its head, and she decides to take the helm and see if she can't settle things down a bit. She runs all over the ark seeking the steering wheel that controls the rudder. Finally, she screams out to Noah, "How do you steer this thing?"

Then perhaps comes Noah's humble reply, "God didn't tell me that. He never said I would steer the ark."

Boom! There it is!

In all the specifications of the ark, God never told him to give it a rudder or a wheel. There was no way for them to guide the direction of the ark—all that was left to the hand of God. By faith, Noah left this journey to God. He did not try to figure out how to add in a way to control the ark's direction. He simply followed the directions exactly as they were given.

What about you? Are you following the directions God has given you in both the mountaintop times as well as in the valley when He seems so far away? Or are you looking for a way to steer your own life when, in fact, God has asked you to simply wait on Him and allow Him to complete the work?

Don't confuse God with Google, expecting an instant answer and completely clear directions. "Okay, God, I need directions from my location to your location." Then we want to see a full printout of those directions with turn-by-turn instructions. We don't get a play-by-play printout of our lives. What we do get is a life filled with hope when we follow His instructions step by step by faith.

The silence of God does not define your relationship with Him, but your reaction to the silence will. Be very careful in the silent times to *cling* to His Word, to *rest* on the promises you have already been given, and to give Him *praise* for the answer that is coming. Respond to His silence with *great expectation*!

Just Stand

God uses various ways speak to us. We must stay close to Him and follow Him to hear His voice. After we have prayed for God to shine His light on us and to reveal anything hidden that may be hindering our line of communication, we may still find He is sometimes silent. This is when we must square up our shoulders and live out Ephesians 6:13: "Therefore put on the full armor of God, so that when the day of evil comes, you may be able to stand your ground, and after you have done everything, to stand."

We must hold on to our faith and keep moving forward in it. We must keep our faith strong, even when we feel as if we are walking through the darkest valley of our lives. We must trust that He is in command. Deuteronomy 31:6 says, "Be strong and courageous. Do not be afraid or terrified because of them, for the Lord your God goes with you; he will never leave you nor forsake you." He reminds us of this again in Hebrews 13:5.

During times when we don't hear God's voice, I love to look for Him in other ways. He is the master at speaking to us without words! Even with rainbows as Genesis 9:16 promises, "Whenever the rainbow appears in the clouds, I will see it and remember the everlasting covenant between God and all living creatures of every kind on the earth."

I can only imagine that Noah and his family may have feared a future destruction by flood after surviving that horrific flood that destroyed so much. It would be only natural to be scared when torrential rains came again. But God made a covenant with Noah that He would not destroy the earth by flood again. Noah knew that God was in control, and he would be safe no matter how bad the storm got. Every time you see the rainbow in the sky, it is not just a beautiful sight to behold, but it is a reminder of a promise made thousands of years ago that still stands today.

Scripture Focus

And He said unto them, "This kind can come forth by nothing, but by prayer and fasting." (Mark 9:29 KJV)

Then the Lord replied: "Write down the revelation and make it plain on tablets so that a herald may run with it. For the revelation awaits an appointed time; it speaks of the end and will not prove false. Though it linger, wait for it; it will certainly come and will not delay." (Habakkuk 2:2–3)

Wait for the Lord be strong and take heart and wait for the Lord. (Psalm 27:14)

Challenge

Do you struggle during times of silence? How do you respond?

Has God spoken to you about something in the past, as He did about my dad, but has been silent since?

I challenge you to get alone with God, pray, and to allow time for Him to speak to you. Remember, God created us with one mouth and two ears. Could it be He wants us to listen twice as much as we speak?

Challenge Accepted

I will create a daily time and a place to quiet myself before the Lord.

What have you prayed and waited on God for specifically?

How will you cling to the promise given? What will you do as you wait on the fulfillment of a promise given?

Will You Pray with Me?

> *Father God*, thank you for the silent times in my life. I know you are still at work in my life. Thank you for the quiet times when I can steal away and sit at your feet and worship you for who you are and simply say thank you for loving me so much. Help me to have faith like Noah, to simply hear your instructions and carry them out without hesitation, even if you don't speak to me again about this matter. I surrender my all to you today and trust you are already at work on my behalf. In Jesus's name, amen.

EIGHT

STAND ON HIS WORD AND LOOK
FOR HIM EVERYWHERE

Shepherd Ray Carman loves shepherding. In his *En-joy the Shepherd* devotional of January 25, he tells of the joy of sitting down out in the field on an old, upside-down white bucket and having one of his sheep join him. He says, "I cannot express to you how relaxing that time is for me as a shepherd. So much of a shepherd's time is taken up with tending fences, checking water supplies, making sure the grass is plentiful, and insuring that no one is sick. When you can just sit and relax in the field with the sheep, it is simply amazing." He continues, "Even better is when one of your sheep loves you and trusts you enough to come and let you run your fingers through their wool/hair. But for that to happen, the sheep has to ignore every built-in instinct he or she has because by nature they are skittish and prefer to stay away from people."

I love the connection these words describe; they are a great reminder of God's love for us. How I'd love to be able to lean into my Father's arms and feel Him running His fingers through my hair. No words needed, just a loving touch. A simple encounter, yet potentially life changing.

I wonder if sheep are like my dogs that respond to touch just as if you were speaking to them and lavishing them with high praises? I wonder if the sheep know how much they are loved when they feel the shepherd's hand on them? What an incredible bond of trust is formed between the sheep and their shepherd.

Can You Feel Him?

I want to share a few ways our sisters and brothers in Christ have felt and seen God speaking instead of hearing Him speak. I pray these true stories provide even greater insight to the depth of His love for you and help you to sense His presence too.

Danielle was involved in a car accident, and the force of the impact caused her seatbelt to break. She said, "I felt myself starting to lift out of the seat as my car was flipping, and I just screamed out to God to help me. Suddenly, I felt pressure, like someone was sitting on me, and I was pushed against my seat. When the rescue squads arrived on scene, they said they thought they were going to have to do a body recovery."

The car had ignited and was burning, but she was able to crawl out through a window to safety. Her injuries were a few cuts and scrapes and one slightly fractured rib. Danielle praises God for responding to her cry for help and keeping her from harm.

Psalm 91:10–12 says, "No harm will overtake you, no disaster will come near your tent. For he will command his angels concerning you to guard you in all your ways; they will lift you up in their hands, so that you will not strike your foot against a stone." Verses 14 and 15 say, "'Because he loves me,' says the Lord, 'I will protect him, for he acknowledges my name. He will call on me, and I will answer him; I will be with him in trouble, I will deliver him and honor him.'"

Beth shared an incredible story of love and faith in her heavenly Father as she recalled the details of a day in 2008 that forever changed her life. She had been trying to reach her husband to find out why their son was not in school. Unable to contact him, she became concerned. "I jumped in my car and headed, a little too fast, to go see my husband at home. I got to a corner, and I just knew I was not going to make the turn. I cried out for Jesus to help me make it. I felt everything lighten up for me as I made my way around the corner. The Lord kept me from seeing the nightmare that I was coming up on until the car was fully stopped and I was getting out. It was then that I noticed my husband's truck was there, but the house had burned completely to the ground. All I could do was scream."

Beth said, "I thank the Lord every day for keeping me strong enough to get there safely that day. I suddenly found myself all alone with my daughter as my husband and my son both died in the fire that day. Every night I would pray that God would keep my son and daughter safe. Then my son died. I was never angry at God for taking my son, I just wondered why He didn't keep him safe.

"Then I had a dream one night, and God used that dream to show me He had indeed kept him safe. God showed me they were both sound asleep when the fire broke out, and they never knew what happened. How awesome to think that you lie down to go to sleep and you wake up in heaven."

"He speaks in dreams, in visions of the night, when deep sleep falls on people as they lie in their beds" (Job 33:15 NLT).

I have a beautiful, Spirit-filled friend who has battled depression on and off for years. Before I share her story, please let me say: Depression is in no way indicative of your spiritual life. The truth is, everyone's struggle in life is different. Depression is ugly and often misunderstood. Sometimes we allow ourselves to get into a funk, and we simply choose to stay there. But others battle daily with emotional and mental health issues not of their own doing; these are issues far above my education and understanding.

Joy shares her incredible story of God's enveloping love.

"I remember the day well. It was Christmas Eve 2002, and I was close to an emotional/mental breakdown. Nothing was going right. I had two miscarriages earlier in the year, and I was so depressed I didn't even want to go to our Christmas Eve service at church that evening. But I did go, and I am so glad I did.

"Following the service, the entire church went to the local Chinese restaurant for dinner. While there, I began to talk with my doctor, and I told him that I was losing it, and I thought I needed help. We talked, and he offered a prescription to me that he felt would help the current situation.

"After dinner, we walked out into the parking lot, and it was snowing. Not just snow, but the most beautiful, peaceful snow I have ever experienced in my life. It was quiet, peaceful, and beautiful—it was God. I truly felt His presence like I had not felt in a very long time. It was a hug; it was His arms around me telling me, I'm still here. I haven't left. This is hard, but we will get through it.

"It is hard to describe in mere words. My family and I went home, and I put our tiny, one-foot-tall Christmas tree out and hung stockings for the kids. I had not done anything else to recognize the holiday up to that point, and now Christmas was here. The next morning was so different. I hadn't been *cured* of my depression, but I had a hope I hadn't had in months. That night was a turning point in my life."

A few weeks later Joy discovered she was expecting again. She gave birth to a bouncing baby boy and would do the same again just two years later.

In the span of four short years, Joy lost two children to miscarriage and all three of her grandparents with whom she had spent her entire life. These grandparents provided her "more emotional support than even her parents," as they were dealing with their own issues. Those four years were the darkest and most difficult she had ever gone through. And yet she says, "To this day, when we have a snowfall like that I get chills, and I am gently reminded of God's unending love, His gentleness through our horrible moments and years."

This story reminds me of Psalm 91:4: "He will cover you with his feathers, and under his wings you will find refuge; his faithfulness will be your shield and rampart."

The Lord blanketed Joy and pulled her close, and she found refuge in His arms. God never spoke a word to her, but she received His message of love.

Have you ever had an experience like those of my friends? Did you recognize it at the time? Or did it occur to you later that you had experienced what I call a kiss from the King—a moment when He shows up in unexpected ways and speaks to us through nature, dreams, feelings, and friends? Those, too, are ways that we can hear the voice of God speaking to us.

I pray you have been able to hear His voice. If you have not, keep listening. Often, we do not hear because we simply do not listen and don't take time to just sit at the feet of the Father and really allow ourselves to just be in His presence.

Many are familiar with the words of Isaiah 40:31 (KJV), "They that wait upon the Lord shall renew their strength." Those who *wait* shall be renewed. Sometimes we just need to sit at His feet and *wait* for that answer to come, whether it be a voice, a nudge through Scripture, a dream, or the counsel of a friend. It can even be a feeling of peace that floods your soul and reminds you God has all the answers you seek, even though you do not. Even in that very instant, He is at work on your behalf.

Will You Pray with Me?

> *Father God,* thank you for each person who has taken time from their lives to read the words on these pages. Would you anoint their time with you as they seek you today? Speak to them however you choose. Use the words you have given me to enrich the journeys of each of these readers and strengthen and encourage them along the way. Draw them closer to you than ever before. In Jesus's name, amen.

TAKE A WALK WITH ME

I once attended a workshop at a women's conference, and the leader led us on walk in the woods. I will never forget what I learned that day as I sat in my chair and met Jesus face to face, even if only in my spirit.

As we close our time together, I would like to ask you to take a walk with me.

Allow your mind to imagine the scene as you read the following words. Allow your heart to feel and receive all the beauty I will describe to you. If you will take this exercise seriously, you will hear the voice you so desperately long to hear.

It's a beautiful day. The sun is shining, and a gentle breeze is blowing; the weather is nearly perfect as we head out toward a wooded area. Walking in the woods is always a new adventure as nature is constantly changing. As some things die, new life springs up all around.

As we head down a trail into the woods, the temperature feels cooler. As we walk, we see little squirrels chasing one another, first up one tree and then back down and over to another tree. They seem not even to notice we have entered their playground as they frolic about, fluffy tails high.

We pause and take a deep breath in through our noses and out through our mouths. Ah! The cleansing breath of nature.

As we move forward, tiny branches break, and leaves crunch under our feet. We touch a tree and feel the softness of the green moss under our hands. As we look up into the tree, its height is almost dizzying. The sun streams through the breaks in the trees and shines on our faces. We see a doe and her fawn playing in the distance. The doe hears us and freezes in her tracks. She nudges her baby as if to protect her, and they go deeper into the woods.

This day is so beautiful and so full of new life. Wildflowers are strewn along the path in brilliant purples, reds, yellows, and oranges. Bright green foliage dances all around us, some with broad leaves and some with smaller ones. We look up just in time to see a mama bird feeding her young in the nest of a tall oak tree. New life, new promises!

You point over to the left, and we get very still and quiet. You think you hear running water, and we pause. Do we dare get off our path and walk toward the sound to see what is there? Or do we stay on the chosen trail; after all, we know where this one leads. What if we get lost? With a little encouragement, we agree nothing ventured, nothing gained, so we set off in search of the water.

We continue moving through the woods, now a little more cautiously, no longer on any sort of path. We step over large fallen limbs and move low-lying branches out of our way. The sound of the water is louder and seems to be crashing against something. A small clearing emerges ahead. Still moving gingerly through what is now thicker forest, we make our way to the clearing. When we finally look up, we are in awe at the beautiful scene spread before us.

The sound of water comes from a swollen creek, its banks covered in a wide variety of wildflowers in an array of bright colors. Beavers have built a dam, and the water is crashing over the top and making a rushing noise as it falls on the other side in a little waterfall.

It is so peaceful here. The clearing in the trees allows the noon sun to shine down on our faces. We bask in it and listen to the sound of the water then start walking toward some large rocks where we can sit and enjoy all the beauty around us.

But as we move closer to the rocks, we fall silent.

In an instant, without a single word spoken, we fall to our knees as Jesus steps out from behind a large rock and greets us. He calls to us: "Children, I have been waiting for you." He helps us to our feet.

He takes your face in His hands, and He tells you, "It's so good to see you. Will you come sit with me a while?" Taking your hand, He leads you to the smaller of the two stones and says, "Tell me what is on your mind today. I want to know everything going on in that beautiful mind of yours."

Jesus has invited you to come and sit with Him.

Take time to bask in His presence and allow Him to speak to you today.

ABOUT THE AUTHOR

Tammy Wilkinson was born and raised in Indiana, where she currently lives with the love of her life, Paul, and her favorite canines, Sophie Grace and Bella Jane.

She has over twenty years of experience in the nonprofit world where she has devoted much of her time and attention to those with physical needs. She has a heart for serving those who have suffered at the hands of others, from children to teens to adults. She desires to speak life into those who have endured deep hurts and help them transition from victim to survivor and watch them become conquerors through Christ.

On December 14, 2016, God thrust her into the spotlight through a viral Facebook video. She immediately recognized His voice and said yes to the call He placed on her life.

Since that time, she has written *Faint Whispers* to answer the questions so many asked about hearing the voice of God. Also, she has opened her datebook to allow God to use her on a speaking platform, vowing to go wherever He leads.

Tammy says her spiritual gifts are teaching, writing, and faith. She feels these gifts should be used in connection with the armor of God. As a strong activator and communicator, Tammy speaks with boldness and confidence to those around her. Her word pictures will pique your interest and inspire you to act. Never intimidated by strangers, Tammy enjoys meeting new people and finding ways to either learn from them or speak life into them. In her world there are no strangers, only friends she has not met yet.

Tammy's idea of success is not money or prestige but rather using God's Word to speak life into others, watching them transform into people who are excited to embrace life. Tammy is thankful for each opportunity she is given to speak the Word of God no matter how small or large.

"Here am I, Lord; use me."

Connect with Tammy Wilkinson at www.facebook.com/tameroo2.

~~⌒~~ ACKNOWLEDGMENTS ~~⌒~~

Ray Carman, the author of *Enjoy the Shepherd: Daily Lessons from the Sheep*, has been a great blessing to me in the writing of this book. With his gracious permission, I have shared lessons he has learned from the Great Shepherd while working as a shepherd. Ray, thank you so much for allowing me to take a peek into your world and for showing the world the true value of sheep and why God likens us to them so much. May your ministry be richly blessed! I could not have done this without you.

Thank you to those of you who so generously shared personal stories from your own lives and walks with Christ. Your willingness to share a portion of your journey make this book even more personal to the reader. I pray each of you are blessed for your faithfulness to Him. I could not have done this without you.

Words cannot express my heart for Redemption Press publisher Athena Dean Holtz! She believed in me before I did. Thank you for being an encourager to this gal who was "bananas" from the beginning. I could not have done this without you.

To my editor, Sandra Byrd, thank you for getting to know me and then editing this book without changing my "voice." Thank you for all the calls, texts, and emails and for being the calming voice in my panic mode. You have made this journey for Jesus a fantastic experience! I could not have done this without you.

To my Facebook followers, you all have been so good to me with your words of affirmation, your likes, shares, comments, and even the random cards and gifts I have received. Thank you for helping me to find my voice for Jesus. I could not have done this without you.

To my husband, Paul. Thank you for working so many long, hard hours to allow me to take time away from the workforce to complete the project that God called me to. I could not have done this without you.

As you can see, this book is not my own. God called me to this project; I was simply an obedient vessel. He has given special gifts to each of the above and to you,the readers. With willing hearts, we completed the project *together*. Thank you for all your love and support!

ORDER INFORMATION

REDEMPTION
P R E S S

To order additional copies of this book, please visit
www.redemption-press.com.
Also available on Amazon.com and BarnesandNoble.com
or by calling toll free 1-844-2REDEEM.